I Lost My Best Friend Today

Dealing With The Loss Of A Beloved Pet

A Handbook with Stories, Support and Sympathy

Author: Judy H. Wright aka Auntie Artichoke,
Family Relationship Coach and Author
www.AskAuntieArtichoke.com (blog)

Co-Author: Chuck Yockey
www.ChuckYockey.com

Published by:
Artichoke Press LLC
www.ArtichokePress.com

ISBN-13: 978-1481897747

ISBN-10: 1481897748

Limits of Liability

This eBook is designed to provide helpful and useful advice regarding the subject matters covered. It is understood that neither the Authors, nor the Distributors of the book engages in the practice of providing legal, professional, or other legally liable information, counseling or regulations governing such matters. As Legal Regulations may change from area to area, it is understood that the Authors and the Distributors of the eBook specifically disclaim any conceivable liability that might be incurred from the use, application, or recommendation of this book.

The stories, essays and photos which were submitted to the Authors, were given freely and with no compensation beyond a free copy of the eBook and a link to their site, if so desired. By submitting these stories, essays and photos to the Authors, the original owner is giving permission to have them reprinted in this book.

The Authors, nor the Distributors of this book make no representations, warranties, or claims whatsoever regarding accuracy, effectiveness, legality, or completeness of the information in this document.

The Authors and Distributors shall NOT be held liable in any form for any loss or other damages resulting from the use of this eBook.

Any and all links are for instructional purposes only and are not specifically recommended by the authors of this book.

Copyright Notice

Published under the Copyright laws of the Library of Congress of the United States of America by: Judy H. Wright http://www.ArtichokePress.com

Table of Contents

Thank You

Special thanks to all those who contributed their stories and suggestions. This eBook would not have been possible without your guidance and sharing. Some wish to remain anonymous, but most have their contact information at the end of their essay or poem.

I posted a small notice to a few blogs and forums and was amazed at the wonderful stories and photos that came in. It was very humbling to receive such heart-warming tales of pets and their owners and their willingness to share with others.

This was a labor of love, but depending on how it is received, we will continue to do other books that will connect the community. Please send us your stories and we will post them on a blog or in a new book.

With love,
Judy H. Wright
Aka Auntie Artichoke, Author and Keynote Speaker
www.ArtichokePress.com
Finding the heart of the story in the journey of life

I also want to thank everyone who contributed to this book. I was brought to tears while reading the outpouring of love from the contributors as I was reminded of the losses of my dogs.

Your heartfelt stories of the love for your pets gives this book an encompassing warmth for those who are experiencing the same loss you have already endured.

For those of us that understand the relationship we have with our pets are the same as we feel for our best friend or our family, we can empathize with the stories told in this book. It is my sincere hope that everyone who has lost their pet and best friend will find peace and comfort.

Chuck Yockey
www.ChuckYockey.com

By DIPTI VAIDYA, GANNETT

Chapter 1 - Loving, Losing and Letting Go

"Eventually you will come to understand that love heals everything, and love is all there is."

- Gary Zukav

When we lose a pet, friend, parent, child, neighbor or anyone who has brought meaning to our lives, we grieve and mourn. Our heart is sore and our emotions are raw. We feel vulnerable and sensitive to what is said and even more so what isn't said about our loss. We are saddened that we won't have their physical association again in this plane of existence. In other words, we are grieving.

For many people who lose their pets to death, the grief is deeper than it was for the death of a relative or friend. The pet represents complete and unconditional love, unlike many human relationships that carry hidden agendas and old resentments.

Life and death can be mysterious and have many layers of emotions around them. Hidden issues from other experiences may come forth when the heart is raw and open. Grief work is individual and progresses at the pace only you are comfortable with.

While we cannot know exactly how you feel, please know that this community of writers and readers of this book knows how loss feels to them. We want to support and comfort one another as we can.

Please accept the contributions and suggestions with an open heart and attitude. Life is an ongoing process of loss, change and growth. Understanding some of the underlying issues and recognizing that others support you in your journey will help you to grow in inner and outer strength.

Loving

This is one of those anonymous stories that float the Internet, but it really touched my heart. I am sure each one of you can relate to the feelings expressed here.

Puppy Size

"Danielle keeps repeating it over and over again. We've been back to this animal shelter at least five times. It has been weeks now since we started all of this," the mother told the volunteer.

"What is it she keeps asking for?" the volunteer asked.

"Puppy size!" replied the mother.

"Well, we have plenty of puppies, if that's what she's looking for."
"I know...we have seen most of them," the mom said in frustration. Just then Danielle came walking into the office, "Well, did you find one?" asked her mom. "No, not this time," Danielle said with sadness in her voice. "Can we come back on the weekend?"

The two women looked at each other, shook their heads and laughed, "You never know when we will get more dogs. Unfortunately, there's always a supply," the volunteer said.

Danielle took her mother by the hand and headed to the door. "Don't worry, I'll find one this weekend," she said.

Over the next few days both mom and dad had long conversations with her. They both felt she was being too particular. "It's this weekend or we're not looking any more," Dad finally said in frustration. "We don't want to hear anything more about puppy size either," Mom added.

Sure enough, they were the first ones in the shelter on Saturday morning. By now Danielle knew her way around, so she ran right for the section that housed the smaller dogs.

Tired of the routine, mom sat in the small waiting room at the end of the first row of cages. There was an observation window so you could see the animals during times when visitors weren't permitted. Danielle walked slowly from cage to cage, kneeling periodically to take a closer look. One by one the dogs were brought out and she held each one.

One by one she said, "Sorry, you're not the one."

It was the last cage on this last day in search of the perfect pup.

The volunteer opened the cage door and the child carefully picked up the dog and held it closely. This time she took a little longer.

"Mom, that's it! I found the right puppy! He's the one! I know it!" she screamed with joy. "It's the puppy size!"

"But it's the same size as all the other puppies you held over the last few weeks," Mom said.

"No not size ---- the sighs! When I held him in my arms, he sighed," she said.

"Don't you remember? When I asked you one day what love is, you told me love depends on the sighs of your heart. **The more you love, the bigger the sigh!"**

The two women looked at each other for a moment. Mom didn't know whether to laugh or cry. As she stooped down to hug the child, she did a little of both.

"Mom, every time you hold me, I sigh. When you and Daddy come home from work and hug each other, you both sigh. I knew I would find the right puppy if it sighed when I held it in my arms," she said.

Then holding the puppy up close to her face she said, "Mom, he loves me. I heard the sighs of his heart!"

"Life is not measured by the breaths we take, but by the moments that take our breath away."

We know, in our rational mind, that we will probably outlive our pets. I have even heard friends and family say, “Well, I am not going to love this pet so much. It just hurts too much when they die.” That is such a great idea for the head. Too bad, our hearts aren’t listening.

All too soon, we find our pets becoming more and more important. Our pets, even though we think of them as human, live relatively short lives. We need to recognize that in our lifetime we will have the privilege of being owned by many pets.
Our family likes to think that each pet we had and then lost either to death or moving, taught us to be better owners of the next one.

It sometimes feels disloyal to stop remembering as if by thinking of your pet constantly could in some miraculous way, bring them back. We feel, erroneously, that if we “hold on” to the pain forever, we will never forget.

Closing the Chapter on a Favorite Book

In order to bring closure and to demonstrate to our heart, we may need a final goodbye in a memorial way. Not to say goodbye to them, but to the dream that they will be coming back as they were. We may need a ritual or means of recognizing that this important member of our family is no longer physically going to greet us at the door each night.

We are closing a chapter on a very sweet book that taught us a great deal about life, and beginning a new book where we will use the wisdom learned to be a better person.

The first book will always be memorable and filled with funny, warm and joyful sections. Just seeing it on the shelf will remind us how much we enjoyed it, but it will never have the anticipation of the first reading, because we know how it will end.

Bridget

My partner and I lost a 17 year old cairn terrier – Bridget - on January 1st of this year. She was "the heart" of the home, kept us on our regular routines and made sure she was walked and fed at the proper times. She was a love with a personality that reminded us always that she was a proper lady; she began her life as a show dog and won for her breed. We adopted her from the kennel when she was 3. When she came to our home, she barked at the furniture; I even had to show her how to hop up stairs.

We still miss her to this day. We called all our friends to share of her passing which helped us work through the pain. Many of our friends sent us sympathy cards which were very comforting. The tears we shed were numerous; she was an integral member of our family. We had a private ceremony realizing her impact on our lives, her part of our family and her arrival at the "rainbow bridge" where she will greet us when we arrive. She was one of our "fur angels"...and lives on in our lives still to this day.

JoEllen Shannon
SPIRIT WOMEN ASSOCIATES
Social Security Disability Advocacy Services
Author of "Waking Up...Alive"
http://spiritwaves.blogspot.com
http://www.spiritwomenassociates.biz
http://www.prosperityjourney.net
http://www.prosperityjourney.biz
http://tinyurl.com/27dwje

Nancy's Cat

Hi Judy,

I am responding to your request to how to respond to someone who has just lost a pet. Animals can become part of the family and sometimes live a long life, but never as long as we do, so grieving the loss of a pet is something that we have to deal with usually more than once in our lifetime. The difficult part is to deal with the lack of empathy from friends and coworkers who are not animal lovers. Those of us who have been through it don't always know the best thing to say or do, either. I would like to share one of my experiences in hopes of helping someone else in that situation.

I had a particular cat that I was very fond of. At the time, I had 3 children and a very busy life, but this pet was very cuddly and a very possessive animal. She was in good health and only 10 years old. (Many indoor cats live a much longer life) The only symptom that I noticed was that she didn't want to play with me. That's it! (I still can't believe that I took her to the vet with that symptom) They did some tests and discovered that she had cancer. Well because of her age, I decided to do everything that I could. This poor thing had chemotherapy, and two surgeries. After the first round of treatment I really thought that she would recover. But six months and $5,000 later the cancer came back and I had to make the painful decision of putting her to sleep. It was so sad to say good-bye to her. Very few people understood.

During the many visits to the feline oncologist, I read about different breeds of cats. I "fell in love" with the Ragdoll breed. I made a decision that would be the next pet for me. Well I couldn't find a breeder to adopt one right away, but several months later I brought home a new kitten. Although she didn't replace the one that I lost, having another full animal's life to look forward to was exciting to me.

One of the best things that made me feel good when I lost that cat was my vet sent me a condolence card with a donation to Cornell University school of Veterinary medicine in my cat's name! That touched me! The research could help other pet's live longer lives!

Nancy M. Sutherland
http://www.nancysutherland.com

Lessons in Letting Go...From A Little Duck

It's just a duck. How much of a pet can it be? That's what our friends would say to us whenever they heard we had a wild mallard duckling as a pet. All I can say is you'd be surprised.

Only July 20, 1965, my sister, brother and I were playing on the beach when we heard quacking and scuffling behind some rocks. We went to investigate and found a two-day-old, abandoned hatchling and a couple of drakes pecking and beating her with powerful wings. Running off the big ducks and rescuing the baby was easy. Getting up the courage to ask Mommy if we could keep her scared us to death. But Mom agreed, and I think secretly loved the downy little creature as much as we did.

Little Duck quickly became part of our flock, or vice versa. Everywhere we walked, she followed—peeping all the way. We spoon fed her Rice Krispies and baby bananas, but she preferred to steal a bite out of a Hershey bar. She had the run of the house by day and slept in a little, wooden crate at night.

We taught her to fly; more importantly for around our house, we taught her to walk up stairs. She bathed in the tub with us until the soapy water purged her feathers of their natural oils. Knowing that she'd have to return to the wild, we stopped that practice as she could barely stay afloat.

When she would leave was entirely up to Little Duck. She was free to fly whenever we played outside. But for a while it seemed that she might choose to stay forever. So much so that we bought her Christmas stocking and filled it with Hershey bars. Then two weeks before Christmas she suddenly knew it was time to go. She took off and flew out to Whale Rock, a massive silhouette of a whale about 200 feet in front of our home.

The three of us stood on the seawall crying and calling. But nature proved stronger, which our parents reminded us was exactly as it should be. Her natural instincts, not our desires, should rule. And just like that Little Duck was gone.

Gradually we accepted our loss and her freedom. Winter was hard, though, as every blast of a duck hunter's gun we heard meant that Little Duck might be dead.

In the end, however, we were rewarded for giving her freedom. She came back in the Spring with her own flock of ducklings. And she kept coming back for six more years.

Kendra Bonnett
Coauthor of Rosie's Daughters: The "First Woman To" Generation Tells Its Story A 2008 IPPY National Book Award winner

Authors/Women Entrepreneurs: Contact me at Two Women Business/Publishing (kendra@twowomenbusiness.com) for effective marketing strategies

Bands/Internet personalities/Businesses looking to reach youth market: Contact me at The Academy Agency (kendra@theacademyagency.com) for management, marketing and media programs and strategies.

Losing and Letting Go

Grief rituals, memorials, funerals and celebrations help everyone to say good-bye to and remember our dear pets in loving, healing ways and to achieve some sense of peace in our hearts.

It may help you to cry the healing tears to have a memorial service and gather friends and family to share tender, funny stories about the deceased.

Isabella

Judy,

Thank you for this outlet. I'm nearing the third anniversary of the death of my sweet girl Isabella, a black Chihuahua. (I've attached one of my favorite pictures.)
She made a profound impact on my life, and I still miss her everyday.

In June 2005, I came home during my lunch break to discover a house fire in my Uptown Dallas townhome. The fire fighters found Isabella's nearly lifeless body in an upstairs bedroom. After four painful, wait-and-see days at the emergency vet, we accepted that her little lungs couldn't fight any more. We agreed with the doctor's recommendation to put Isabella to sleep. Surrounded by my husband and my best friend, I cradled her in my arms, kissed her head and spoke softly to her while she drifted off to a peaceful slumber.

The days that followed were some of the most painful I've known. I've lost relatives and friends, yet some how, losing Isabella was different. I felt grief and sadness for sure, but I also felt guilt. Guilt that I wasn't able to better protect her, this small, sweet devoted little creature. I sought solace in others' favorite memories of Isabella. I pored over every picture I ever snapped. And I looked for books that granted me permission to grieve "just a dog." The Loss of a Pet, by Wallace Sife was the light during those darkest days. His writings gave me permission to feel the emotions that may have seemed irrational to others, and he helped me understand that animals do not fear death like most people do. It was infinitely helpful to think Isabella left this world unafraid of what would come next.

In the years following her death, we adopted two more Chihuahua babies. They do not replace Isabella. Another dog never will. But, they remind me how to love unconditionally, something Isabella first taught me. Her pictures still grace mantels and book shelves in our house, and my husband and I still share our favorite Isabelly stories - like how she was the world's best napper, or how she would gracefully stretch her long, lean body like a ballerina every morning as she waited for breakfast. She was a dear friend, my first baby and so much more than "just a dog."

Judy, I hope you have a box of tissues nearby. I can't imagine the bittersweet stories you'll read as you work on this piece! There seems to be something about animal lovers... Again, thank you for the opportunity to share my story. Even three years later, it is therapeutic to talk about her.

Good luck, and best wishes,

Jessica Newell
Dallas, TX

It is not the attachment and love of our pets that causes our heart to break when that inevitable loss comes. It is the detachment or letting go that is so painful..

I have always enjoyed the image presented by John-Roger in Life 101 of putting your hand in a bucket of water. When you remove your hand from the water the hand leaves no impression. He says that there are those that maintain the reason the hand leaves no trace in the water is because the water is not attached to the hand.

On the contrary, while the hand is in the water, it is surrounded, enfolded, embraced and caressed by the water. When the hand is removed, it still has some remnants of the water, but the hand could no more hold the water than the water could hold the hand. When the time comes to move on, it is important to move on while retaining the memory of the exquisite life experiences.

"It is one of life's laws that as soon as one door closes, another opens. But the tragedy is that we look at the closed door and disregard the open one."

- Andre Gide

Photo courtesy of livinghealthytechniques.com

Chapter 2 - What Having Pets Can Teach US

"Hurry, Mom, come and look." Said little James when he saw his first snake. "Here is a tail wagging without any dog on it."

- Art Linkletter

As a parent educator, I encourage parents who did not receive great relationship training in their youth to look to animals as mentors. If more parents would greet their children at the door with love and acceptance in their eyes, their whole being expressing eagerness to be touched, patted and played with, family relationships would grow to a new level.

A pet's non-verbal language is unconditional love and forgiveness. Their love is not dependent on grades, promotions, or soccer scores. Even if you were grouchy yesterday, they forgive easily.

They are loyal, funny, kind, and irreverent like you wish you could be in public, trusting, reliable, dependable, and love to play games, easily satisfied and great listeners. They never share your secrets or judge you. They tolerate your idiosyncrasies and put up with your moods. All in all, they are great friends and companions.

We form interdependent relationships with our pets. They may depend on us for food, lodging, occasional hug or trip to the vet. But we depend on them to be our best friends.

No wonder we miss them when they are gone.

I have included an article I wrote for a magazine a few years ago. Hope you enjoy it.

The Health Benefits of Owning Pets

By Judy H. Wright (2006)

There is strong evidence (as reported in The Book of Inside Information) that owning and caring for pets has numerous health and happiness values. Even though those of us who own pets know the comfort and companionship they bring, now we have scientific evidence that reinforces that attachment. A recent study shows that of patients hospitalized for heart attacks, those who owned pets were far more likely to survive past the first year than those who did not.

Another test done on post-coronary patients showed that of 39 who did not own pets, 11 died the first year. Of 53 who did own pets, only three died the first year. Subsequent tests showed that having a dog, which might have provided additional exercise was not the determining factor. The main reason listed was simply having and loving a pet.
The companionship that comes from caring for a responsive animal like a cat, dog or bird will decrease the sense of isolation that comes with those who live alone or must come home to an empty house. "Latch-Key" children, whose parents do not get home from work for some time, feel a sense of responsibility as well as comfort in hurrying home from school to care for their pet.

Knowing that there is someone there eager to greet them and offering a encouraging lick on the cheek or a wagging tail can be a welcome distraction. Touching and caressing an animal act as an anti-anxiety agent as well as easing feeling of helplessness or depression.

Owning a dog lessens fear of defenselessness and encourages going out of doors for sunshine and exercise. Feeling safer is a positive health benefit for everyone.

The sense of unconditional love that comes with a pet is never overrated by the pet owner. It fills a basic human need to love and be loved. So hug your pet, talk to him, buy special toys and treats and don't feel guilty.

You will both benefit physically, emotionally and spiritual from the relationship.

Abigail - Best Dog in the World

© Connie Ragan Green

Abigail was the best dog in the world. You may think I am just saying this because she was my dog, but it was common knowledge to anyone who knew her.

I was first diagnosed with cancer back in 1992. I had a little Yorkie at the time, Mickey, but she was stubborn and had a mind of her own. I loved Mickey very much, but we just did not have the relationship I had had with other dogs in my life.

It was while I was undergoing therapy that I first found out about Abigail. Her owner was my physical therapist, John. John and his wife had three children under the age of six, and Abigail was a sixty pound Basset Hound. They had added her to their family a year earlier, when she was just a puppy, but now that she was full grown it just wasn't a good fit for the family. When the found out they were going to have to move from their house into an apartment, it was time to find Abigail a new home.

Abigail and I first met when I went to visit John and his family. There were packing up their belongings, and she just knew something was not right. When I showed up with my five pound Yorkie, she tried to hide behind the big chair in the living room. Because of her size, hiding was not going to work. She slowly came over to me, and I fell in love.

I learned that Abigail had been used to the three children climbing all over her. The youngest one, not quite two years old, was used to pulling on her long, floppy ears, and Abigail had never once complained. She looked up at me with big, sad eyes, and I imagined she was wondering how many children I might have at my house. When Mickey and I got up to leave, Abigail got up and walked to the door with us, as if she knew she now belonged to me.

Abigail loved living at my house. Mickey was there, barking at every sound, but there were no children and I was sick in bed much of the time. She wanted to get in the bed with me, but at sixty pounds it was like having another person. She resigned herself to the fact that the dog bed next to me would have to suffice.

Mickey died of heart failure the following year, so it was just Abigail and I for many years. She went swimming in my neighbor's pool, rode in the car, and got special treats whenever I went out for dinner.

As she aged, Abigail began to slow down quite a bit. I finally decided to get her a personal trainer, and that was when I brought Jack, a black and tan dachshund, into the family. Jack was blind and Abigail was not very nice to him at first. She would bark to make him turn his head, and then she would gobble down his food.

Then Jack made himself at home by sleeping on her "big girl bed", and she stared at him with disgust. She gave me a look that said, "Can't you just take him back? Tell them we don't want him anymore."

But Jack stayed, and soon they were inseparable. They chased each other in the back yard, and Abigail slept next to her bed, allowing Jack to sleep there, perched upon her big bed like a little king. She would leave part of her food for him, and even allowed him to bite on her ears, perhaps reminding her of the children she used to live with.

Jack was doing his job as a personal trainer, and Abigail was like a puppy again, at least for the next few years.

Two years ago, when Abigail was twelve, she was diagnosed with stomach cancer. Even though she had been there for me during my cancer treatment, I had promised myself that I would never put a beloved pet through this kind of treatment, especially when it would only prolong her life. There was no cure, and over the next two weeks she became progressively worse.

It would have been cruel and selfish of me to put her through any more pain. So for the first time in my life I was the brave one, and held her close as the vet gave her the final shots. She looked into my eyes until they glazed over, and then she was gone.

Abigail was a part of my life for eleven years. During that time I had cancer twice, and we also went through the earthquake that hit Los Angeles in 1994. Now you can see why she was the best dog in the world.

Connie Ragen Green
http://www.EbookWritingandMarketingSecrets.com
Join me on a Free weekly teleseminars

Blackie

Blackie, a not very original name for a scrawny black cat, came to us from my wife's ex-husband. He was only five pounds and very dirty, with some kind of auto-immune disease that attacked his gums making it difficult for him to eat. We nursed him back to health though over the next three years of his life, but we could never beat the disease despite steroid treatments, acupuncture, herbs, and holistic medicine. We would try anything to help him. He put on some weight and then have a flare-up and lose most of it.

Because I was allergic to cats, my whole life I have been cat-phobic. To combat my allergies, we installed air filter machines in all the rooms of the condo, and ran them around them clock. I put up with the sneezing and discomfort because this cat was just the sweetest little animal. When I came home at night from work, he would follow me upstairs. I lay down to rest before dinner and he would climb on my chest and lie there, purring, while I petted him. When my wife and I sat on the sofa to watch television, he stretched out between us, putting his back paws on her leg, and his front paws on my leg, always in physical contact with us.

The lesions in his mouth spread to his throat and stomach and he could no longer eat anything. We pureed and strained vegetables with meat broth to try to get him some nourishment but it was no use. We couldn't let "the little man", as I called him, suffer any longer. As he sat calmly in my wife's lap, purring away while I stroked his back, the vet administered an overdose of anesthetic, and in a few seconds, he was gone. I'm surprised by how much I miss him. To remember him, and honor his memory, I put his picture from when he came to us on the cover of my first collection of fiction, Hunger and Other Stories. In the picture, he's on a patch of carpet and I know that any second, he's coming over to sit in my lap.

Ian Randall Wilson
Author of Hunger and Other Stories
http://www.hollyridgepress.com

One of the favorite books I have read and shared with my grandchildren is Jane Goodall's *The Ten Trusts-What We Must Do to Care For the Animals We Love. I quote from the Fourth Trust-Teach Our Children to Respect and Love Nature.*

> *Children brought up in a caring family that respects animals, especially when those children grow up in close contact with some animal, tend to be kind to animals as adults and to be loving and compassionate individuals. When children from seemingly normal homes show extraordinary cruelty toward animals, it may indicate some serious psychological disturbance.*
>
> *Children's relationships to animals, then, can be a means of teaching compassion and kindness or, alternatively, an indicator, when those qualities are lacking and abuse of animals is present, of potential psychological problems.*

Our pets symbolize so many things to each of us. Many of my single friends think of their pets as children and expect those of us who love them to also accept and love their pets, just as they do our children.

Muffie

Last April, my 14-year old German Shepherd, Muffie, started to falter. In weeks, she went from my energetic, gentle giant to a dog who couldn't even walk to her beloved backyard. My husband and I made the heart wrenching decision to put her to sleep. We stayed with her while the injection was given, and we cried like babies. My daughter was away at school, so I had to call and tell her that her best bud was gone.

A week later, my husband came across this puppy who looked so much like Muffie. She had the same black and brown coloring and she just looked like she belonged to us. We went to the shelter where she was and I picked her up and I knew she was mine. What we didn't know was that this little pup had Parvo. We found a great vet hospital that vowed to treat her until there was nothing more they could do.

We visited her every day and I kept telling Frankie Muffie (that's what we named her) that Muffie was looking out for her and she wanted her to be with us for a long time. The vet said it was a miracle but this little puppy rebounded and grew into a huge 72 pound shepherd/lab mix. This needy little puppy would never have found us had it not been Muffie's time to go.

Muffie's passing opened us up to a new puppy who needed us too. We will always love our Muffie and know that in some way, she sent Frankie to us too. We still joke to this day, that Muffie saw Frankie in the light and told her to "Go back and be well. That house is a good gig!"

Donna Cavanagh
http://www.PossessionPoints.com

PS: The first one is Muffie, my German Shepherd, who passed away with our other dog LuLu. The second photo is of Frankie Muffie, the pup who came to us soon after Muffie died with LuLu.

I would like to end this chapter with an essay that was submitted for an earlier book called *Caution without Fear-Safeguarding Children from Sexual Abuse*. The author, who has asked to remain anonymous, is sharing what it was like to grow up in a sexually abusive home and how much animals meant to her.

Animals Saved My Sanity

Like most children who've been molested, I withdrew from everyone, seeking my solace in nonhuman form. Leafy hideouts provided a haven. Animals became my confidants and friends. Human beings, including parents, siblings, and peers comprised a world apart from me, one I could only observe from my invisible existence, but to which I could never belong.

There are two obvious reasons for this. 1) Perpetrators of sexual abuse prey on the child who craves love and attention and who has a low self-esteem. 2) When violated, the child feels dirty, ashamed, and guilty.

This shame drives them to seclusion. He or she wants to hide because she feels so dirty that she fears people will be able to tell just by looking. He wants to be alone, for he feels undeserving of love.

When a child hides in a closet covering herself with piles of blankets or clothing, and stays there for hours or until discovered and dragged out, suspect sexual abuse. Other hiding places such as an empty box, a crawl space, a thicket, or even the top of a tree may indicate trauma.

A child may gravitate to animals to provide the affection and protection that a child naturally needs. A horse will not tell your secrets to anyone. A dog will never tell you that it was your fault.

A kitten won't call you a liar. Please allow children their pets—and their privacy.

It may be all that keeps them from utter despair. A child without anyone to turn to may become suicidal when feeling utterly without hope of redemption.

Love, trust, respect, and honesty are the best preventative measures a parent or caregiver can bestow on a child.

Love, trust, respect, and honesty are the best tools for allowing a violated child to open up to you and get help. Never ridicule them for their isolating behavior.

Never deprive them of the solace they find in nature and animal friends.

Anonymous

My friendship with Mitzi was like the friendship that many children have with their pets. My mother and father thought it was "good for me" to have a dog for a companion. Well it was good for me, but it was only many years after she died that I began to understand how good it was, and why.

- Fred Rogers (Mr. Rogers)

Chapter 3 - Unexpected Loss of a Pet

"Your pain is the breaking of the shell that encloses your understanding."

- Kahlil Gibran

Sometimes we know when death is approaching and we can prepare. We have time to say goodbye and let best animal friend know we will always remember them.

But, many times the loss comes from an accident or the pet may have been stolen or run away. As we have seen as landlords, pets are not allowed in rental units and must be given away. It is hard on families to unexpectedly loose their friend.

In these situations, there is usually no immediate "closure" and the owner may suffer pangs of guilt or remorse, even if the situation could not have been avoided.

Right after our granddaughter Melissa shared the story of Peter, her puppy who died, she called in tears. The two remaining puppies were gone. Not from death or disease like Peter but simply disappeared.

Her Mom had put them out at 5:45 am and watched them frolic on the front yard with Sibrika and Sonic, the Icelandic Shephard parents. After showering, she opened the door to let them in and only Sibrika and Sonic were there.

They do not live in a congested city where someone would have stolen them for a puppy mill, but on a remote road in a friendly rural community. The family has searched now for over a week, as have neighbors and friends. They just seemed to have disappeared. The Fish and Wildlife officers thought it unlikely a Mountain Lion would have taken them both, especially when there were chickens nearby.

The extended family and network of friends is sending positive thoughts, prayers and good wishes as the family continues to search every abandoned barn, culvert, cave and area where they could be.

As Melissa shared in her essay: "It is good not to be sad alone."

Bailey

Hello,

We lost our dog, Bailey, two years ago this July. She was a 7 year old German Shepherd who had been in excellent health. She got diagnosed with a lung infection for which steroids were prescribed - the only option to save her life. The side effects of the steroids ended up killing her. We took her to the vet for a check up and they said she was doing better. A few days later, I came home and she would not come inside from the outside patio. My husband came home, and with a neighbor, carried her into the car as she could not walk. They rushed her to the vet, who told us she was in septic shock.

The vet was just closing, but they stayed open to give her an IV. They sent us an hour away to the nearest vet emergency clinic. By the time we got there, she was deeper in shock. The vet examined her and told us that she was going to pass any time. We chose to have her injected to make it painless and quick. We had our young daughter with us, so we took a moment to say good-bye. Then my daughter and I left and my husband stayed with her to hold her as she passed on.

Friends and family sent cards and brought flowers. Everyone knew how much we were grieving. The vet at our clinic that gave her the IV, sent us a full page letter about what a great dog we had and how sorry she was. It really touched us.

A photographer friend made us a photo tribute, which another friend had framed for us. Our friends were wonderful. We made a rose garden memorial and a few friends and neighbors sent us rose bushes for it.

With our young daughter, we did a few things. We got a few books from the library about pet death, which was very helpful. We also bought a balloon and let it go up to heaven to be with Bailey. She drew a lot of pictures of it and we still talk about our pup almost daily.

Sincerely,

Meagan Farrell
Clear the Clutter
(360) 631-7268
clear_theclutter@yahoo.com
http://cleartheclutterprofessionalorganizing.blogspot.com/

Cathy's Loss

Hi Judy,

I wasn't sure which story to tell. None of these 4 losses were at all typical. My girls were Meg, Chelsea, Iris and Mollie. Meg and Mollie were barely 2 years old (both border collies). Iris, a Great Pyrenees was about 5. And, Chelsea was just a bit older than Iris and also a Pyrenees.

All four of my girls died within 3 years of each other. Meg was hit by a car where I was close enough to hear. Chelsea had been tied up in a neighbor's yard with little care and less grooming. I was bathing her when I discovered multiple masses on her chest. Iris, having been gone about 3 days, I found shot in the chest. And, Mollie was just 18 months when my husband (a veterinarian) diagnosed her with bone cancer.

Honestly I didn't know where to start. I did notice on your web page that you were a coach. So am I. I was going to my third week-end intensive on Process Coaching (CTI). Meg died the day before. I could have rescheduled. But, I decided not to. Instead, on the first full day, I volunteered to be in a coaching demo and was coached around the loss of Meg. The effect Meg had on me, (she was truly my love) her death and what happened that Saturday morning has had a greater impact on my life than almost anything else I've ever experienced.

- Cathy Jansen

Scout

Scout was a 5 year old male Dalmatian when he first came into our lives. My daughter and went to the Humane Society and saw him for the first time. He was the only dog not jumping up and barking-but I remembered his eyes. We went back the next day. He had been neglected, starved and beaten.

We fell in love. He was my constant companion. He never left my side. I was forever tripping over him. I would call for him not realizing he was standing right next to me. My neighbors got the biggest kick out of him because when I mowed the lawn he was right there walking with me.

When he was eight we discovered he had congestive heart disease. He took all his pills twice a day like a trooper until the day he died. Having a bad heart never slowed him down-he would run and run through the hills of Blue Mountain-one of his favorite places. By the time he was 13 years and 9 months he was very frail-he had been sick for some time. My sister and I took him to his vet and it was time. That day was truly one of my saddest moments. Scout was cremated. I have scattered his ashes all over Montana-in his favorite camping and walking spots and in all my flower gardens.

I received many cards and phone calls as the news spread of Scout's passing. My co-workers are all animal lovers and they hugged me – gave me wonderful cards and talked and understood. Having so much love and support from family and friends helped me through my grief. There is not a day that goes by that I don't think about him. I have my favorite picture of him at work and at home. My friends and family still share stories of Scout-he was well-loved -and he had a great sense of humor. I feel so blessed to have had him in my life. He was a great friend and comrade. At times my heart aches but even when I feel sad his memory always makes me smile.

In loving memory,
Cynthia Daniell

I was impressed with a letter to the editor recently written by a woman I had not seen for years. When I called to tell her I would like to include her story in this book, she was very pleased to share.

Her story of loss reinforces the value of assuming responsibility for your pet by not only feeding, but training and controlling their actions as much as possible.

Accidents happen. Sometimes, as Harold Kurshner said in his wonderful book *Why Do Bad Things Happen to Good People* it is just being in the wrong place at the wrong time. There is no divine plan to hurt or put in harm's way our beloved friends. Unfortunately, it is just the way the cookie crumbles, the rain falls, animals get out and accidents happen.

As animal owners, we learn and go forward with a renewed appreciation of the time we had with our pet. Gail is angry and rightfully so.

Anger is the basis for all change in the world. Knowing Gail, she will channel that anger into activism and community education. She will not turn it inward and allow it to destroy her heart and soul. Latte would not have wanted that. She will turn it outward and use it as a basis for change. Latte would have wanted that.

Letter to the Editor
Cat Safety/Unruly Dogs
(Death of a Pet)
Gail Miller
15 June 2008

Cat owners, be vigilant. Dog owners, please keep your dogs secure in your yard.

My cats were playing on the front lawn when one of my kitties was brutally picked up and shaken by a cream/white husky dog. was witness to the whole horrifying event, watching my kitty screaming and clawing to get loose. I ran screaming to get the dog away from my Latte. Latte then ran away, dragging his hind legs.

I got the dog into my car and ran to find my injured, terrified kitty, who was crying and trembling as I picked him up to get him to my vet.

I immediately took the dog to Animal Control, which made me angry that the dog had to come before my kitty. I then got my kitty to my vet. The X-rays showed one cracked vertebrae, which was the main culprit. My kitty passed away that night from damage to his spinal cord.

I love animals and have helped many dogs reunite with their owner, who says, “How did they get out?” Most dogs I find rarely have a name tag. The owner says, “I've been meaning to get them” or “My dog just lost them.” I spoke with the owner of the husky, who said, “Oh, it was windy and the gate/door blew open and the dogs got out, my Lab loves cats but not my Husky.”

My beloved kitty, Latte, would still be alive and enjoying his happy, carefree life at my home but for an irresponsible owner who can't keep tags on her dog and who can't keep her dog secured in his fenced yard. Due to this dog owner's negligence, my kitty suffered and died and I am devastated. I am so angry with irresponsible dog owners.

Gail Miller
1721 South 4th West
Missoula, MT 59801
(406) 543-7845

Using an Animal Communicator

(This story was taken from an email to the family)

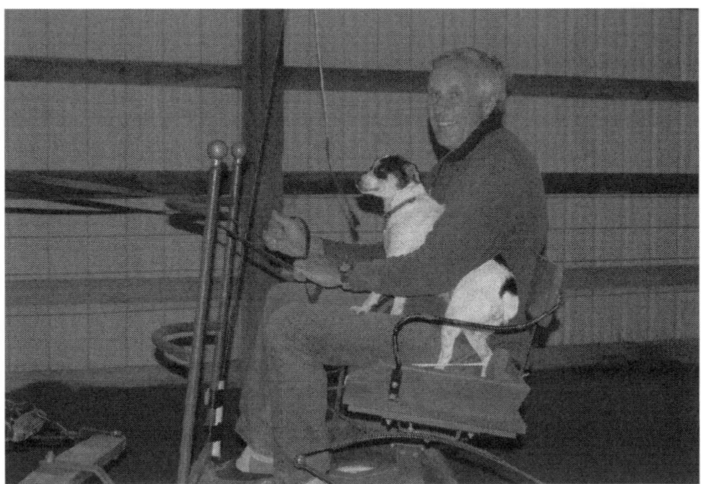

I am so filled with joy and happiness I can barely type. I know most of you didn't know Alex's little Rat Terrier puppy - Lotta Dot - was missing - I just couldn't speak of it to many people not wanting to put out the negative energy. So in brief I will explain.

Alex is in Iowa at the annual draft horse and driving horse sale. His traveling companion is Lotta Dot who has already been across this wonderful country as far as Florida - to PA and back to MT last fall. She is 9 months old but has seen more country than most people!

While Alex was unloading hay at one of the Amish farms, one of the bales rolled close to her which must have scared her and she took off in hiding. When Alex was through with the hay he couldn't find her. He searched, and searched and called and walked around then drove around the Amish community looking for her. He asked every person he saw to let him know if they saw her. Soon the whole community knew Alex was looking for a little rat terrier. Many of the Amish in this area know Alex from the years of buying horses from them and taking horses to them for training. In fact he bought the mother dog to his puppy from this same area.

Alex couldn't stay there looking for his precious puppy - he had to head back to Waverly for the horse sale. The reason he was there was to buy horses. So he spent a lonely and sad night without his puppy partner. The next day he went out to the community again - which is about 40 miles away from the sale grounds. He looked and walked and drove around calling for Lotta. No luck. He had to return to the sale again - business is business.

I contacted my favorite animal communicator in Texas - to see if she would tell the puppy to return to the place she last saw Alex. Unfortunately the communicator didn't have time to devote to helping find lost dogs anymore - but she sent me a link to her site with suggestions on what the owners can do to help.

Here is the link www.katberard.com/com_lost.htm. When Alex had the time to talk on the phone - I read the suggestions to him.

With the help of the article Alex mentally told Lotta to return to the place he last saw her. Then the next thing and the hardest thing to do was to let go. Stop worrying. Trust that the dog will be found. There are many more things to read in the article and Alex did what feltwas right to him.

Later that afternoon, the wife of one of his Amish friends called me saying she saw the puppy! She tried to call to her but the pup was so scared she ran out into the corn stubble.

I was so excited to know she was still around and alive, I called Alex on the cell phone. He had just ordered lunch and ate it in a hurry then drove back out to the Amish community. He called and called but couldn't find her. He searched under the buildings but because the snow was so deep he couldn't see very well. He stayed until dark but didn't find Lotta. So he drove back to Waverly. Knowing she was still in the area, he felt better about her being around and still had hope of finding her but still lonesome and worried about his little frightened dog out in the cold Iowa nights all by herself without much for shelter and little to eat. So Alex mentally told her to go back to the place he last saw her and to trust the people there to help her.

Later that night - one of the Amish boys called me thinking they had Alex's cell number - and said the puppy came back in the yard while they were unloading more hay. She jumped in the truck and sat there. When they took her out of the truck she followed them into the house and went inside. The family knew how important this dog was to Alex so they kept her inside, safe and warm. You have to realize the Amish do not usually allow dogs in their homes.

I was almost in tears when they told me they had the puppy and called Alex right away. He was able to make contact with the young Amish man and arranged to meet with him in Waverly at 4 o'clock the next morning. That is when they would be in town to get horses ready for the sale and they would bring her to him. But the mother of the family did not want to risk having Lotta get away from them and insisted Alex come back there to get her, which, of course, he did.

Lotta was SO happy to see Alex – he called me and said he doesn't need a bath now because his puppy "cleaned him up pretty good!!!"

We both really believe that the mental messages we sent her worked and by ending our fear and worry - this allowed the message to be delivered with a feeling of safety and love - not fear.

Kayo Fraser

www.wildhorsebooks.com
www.drivehorses.com

A dog is the only thing on earth that loves you more than he loves himself.

-Josh Billings

Photo courtesy of animalfixer.com

Chapter 4 - When Cure Turns to Comfort Care

"I wish people would realize that animals are totally dependent, helpless, like children; a trust that is put upon us."

- James Herriot, author of All *Creatures Great and Small*

The following section is taken from a new book that will be published soon by ArtichokePress.com called *When Death is Near-A Handbook for Families Facing the Loss of a Loved One.*

What is Comfort Care?

Comfort care means COMFORT, not cure. Our scientific and medical cultures are trained and geared toward cure, treatment, and results. It is often difficult to move from this modality into comfort care only.

Such things as lab work, blood sugar reading, monitors, antibiotics, artificial nutrition, food and water, meds, continued chemotherapy, insulin and other result and data gathering procedures may need to be questioned as the dying process progresses. We must ask what will truly comfort the dying person, both physically and emotionally and let this guide our actions.

Caring, nurturing and comfort can most often be accomplished without medical procedures or even food and water in most instances. However, if these things comfort a dying loved one it may be beneficial to continue them. Check frequently with the person for any desire for change or requests to discontinue any of these measures.

What is Palliative Care?

End-of-life care is commonly referred to as palliative care. This care is usually done by a team of healthcare professionals, as well as the patient's family. It focuses on management of physical symptoms and emotional support to both the family and the patient.

Usually the over riding goal of palliative care is caring for patients, rather than curing an illness, if there has been a terminal diagnosis.

Choosing palliative care does not mean that patients must stop seeking a cure for their condition.

As death becomes more imminent, attempts to cure the disease taper off, while palliative care measures increase.

We encourage families and care givers to continue acting as advocates for their loved one, to ensure that their needs and wishes are being met and respected.

Tiger

My cat Tiger is five years old. In December 2007 he developed a mass on his neck that my older son found. I took him to the vet and they tried to biopsy it but to no avail. Once it started interfering with his eating about a two months later I took him back to the vet and had them just remove it. They sent it off and it came back malignant-cancer-large cell lymphoma. If I opted to do nothing then he had until June to live- 3 months. I couldn't see spending money for chemo just to extend his life for a few months.

So, June has come and gone and he has deteriorated in the last few days. So... I was told by the vet (who is a good acquaintance of mine). Others acted sympathetic cause Tiger is such a sweet cat. I had many people tell me to go ahead and put him to sleep. My problem is I feel like if I do then I am cutting his life short. However, he is at the point now that I don't think he can really go on. I plan on having him cremated. I will more than likely buy a brick to go into a memorial garden that our vet has.

What has helped me to heal? I think just knowing he will be pain free will give me peace enough. At this point, he has a bad ear infection and the vet gave me antibiotics for him. His head is tilted and cannot walk. I have to pick him up and put him in the litter box for him to use it. He eats maybe once a day. I have watched a lively cat go down to nothing in a couple of weeks. It is extremely sad.

I am not happy because we took him to the vet the day before yesterday to have him put to sleep and the vet convinced me to give him antibiotics for his ear and see if that helps. Good grief! He has cancer! He won't get better. It is hard to convince myself to shove pills down his throat when he doesn't want to move. I think this is all in vain.

Thanks-

Ellen, Tiger's Mom

Maui

My husband said that our dog, Maui, loved me more than anyone else in the world did, even more than he or my mother loved me. I think he was right.

Maui was born in our kitchen, due to us having unknowingly bought a young Norwegian Elkhound who was pregnant. Of the 5 puppies, I picked out Maui to be my special dog. We also kept another of the puppies, Kona. While I always loved Maui, we did not become close until after Kona died when both dogs were four years old. While we were away from home, one day, they had both eaten some surgical soap we left out while preparing a first aid kit. (We found out too late that Physo_Hex soap is poisonous, which is why it is no longer on the market.)

Maui was special in her deep love for me. She waited by the door for me when I was gone. If I were gone more than a few hours, I was greeted with yips and little love bites on my legs and ankles.

When she was 8 ½, we found out she had a urinary cancer. I still feel guilty that we did not recognize it soon enough. We thought it was just an infection. The vet wanted to get a diagnosis to be sure. So, in the process of getting tissue, somehow her bladder became blocked and she could not urinate. Every day for a whole month we went to the vet every morning 7 days a week to catheterize her to release 24 hours of urine.

She was comfortable for a while, then was in pain until the next morning. We kept hoping the chemotherapy drug would help, but it did not. She leaked urine sometimes, so I either put a diaper on her so she could be inside, or slept with her outside on the deck.

She only wanted to be next to me, and I, her.

She was in pain, but did not seem to want to leave me. Finally, we decided we must put her to sleep. We had a great morning with treats, hugs, and taking pictures. The shot acted so fast, she was gone in a minute. 8 ½ years was too short to have dear Maui, the most loving dog I have ever had.

Maui's illness affected others, too. After her death two different vets sent notes and donations in her honor to animal groups. Friends sent cards. But the card that touched us the most was from the veterinarian technician who helped with Maui every day. She said "Maui was a brave little girl and quite a fighter. I will always remember her that way." And so will we.

–Sandy LaForge

Missoula, Montana

Live Harp Music & Animals

I found the following information very interesting for two reasons:

1) Sandy LaForge who shared her story above is a harpist and came here to Montana to study with the Chalice of the Repose, a doctorate school in music thanatology. They were so instrumental in easing the suffering of my mother and the family as she was dying. I still play the cd of harp music to ease stress and relax.

2) Sandy didn't tell me about this, but a friend I found on Facebook, Chris Ann Bowman, who contributed the bonus video and harp music you received when you bought this eBook.

Here is an article of offering harp music to an aging, transitioning animal:
http://www.harpforanimals.com/

And another is here, highlights of info on the page in quote:
http://harpist1.tripod.com/id32.html

In 2001, people began to report that they were using the Harp of Hope CD with their sick or elderly animals, especially to help arthritic dogs fall asleep and to calm agitated cats. Diane, who has fostered almost 40 felines over 12 years for the Humane Societies in Toronto and Minnesota adds, "I routinely use live harp music and the Harp of Hope CD to relax and comfort nervous or post-operative cats. She adopted "Frosty," found near death in a Minnesota minus-20 winter, after using a regimen of harp vibrations to support her healing. This 1 year old female Siamese mix was able to regenerate three frozen extremities which had been scheduled for amputation, and was also found to have regrown necrotic ear tissue and fur which had previously disintegrated. Frosty, now 8 years old, has always shown a marked interest in music, often lying at the foot of the harp while it is being played.

While far less clinical research exists on music and animals, controlled studies are increasing. For example, a pilot study in summer, 2003, on canine patients in a veterinary hospital in St. Augustine, FL reported that dogs who received harp music following surgery showed decreased stress, anxiety, and vocalization, and returned more quickly than the control group to normal respiration. Other studies on cats, cows, rabbits, and horses are emerging with similar positive results. We invite your submission of additional resources or questions to Dr. Schneider at healingharpist@hotmail.com

Here's another resource: http://www.petpause2000.com/harp_therapy_journal.html
So much out there to help our beloved animals.

The Waiting

And here we lie in wait,
with Death Knocking at the Door.

Come In, Come In – it is time.
Why do you hesitate?

The space between Hope and acceptance
is a lingering dread.

Mourning can not begin to heal the pain,
until this Moment has passed.

We wait for the knowing soon to come.
We put on hold our tears.

For the ultimate time of pass has not yet come.
Unfulfilled we wait.

What must yet come?
For what do you Wait?

Has the carriage not passed near
to take you beyond?

Is there someone who is yet to come?
Is there a goodbye not yet said?

We sit with our breath held and Wait,
until the moment has begun.

This time between the acceptance and grief,
of loss and memories Wait.

We give you love, and brush your mane;
and offer our prayer of thanks.

Your life has been dear to us,
and your love for us is not a surprise.

You cared so much for other's life,
and tended to their wounds.

You taught and shared and cared,

it is for you we Wait.

The time will come, there is no doubt,
and loneliness will replace,

This time we offer you in Wait.

May the wings of death take you home,
While in hope to see you again, we Wait.

Kayo Fraser
Feb 4, 2007
www.wildhorsebooks.com
www.drivehorses.com

Chico

"Chico" was a Maine Coon we rescued from a local farm. We weren't as smart as the mother, in that his survival was very unlikely. With much help from our vet, Chico not only survived, but he thrived. Although he had lost his hearing as a result of the many complications at birth, he lived a complete 14 years.

My wife went to California to visit our daughter and Chico began his normal pouting activities: Didn't eat, slept more than usual, wouldn't play with others, and was just a bit ornery. However, after a couple of days, I knew something wasn't right. Our vet ran the usual tests and felt an x-ray was necessary. The x-ray revealed a large tumor.

Over the next two weeks, our friends and family got regular updates as Chico's condition worsened. On the day we put Chico down, two remarkable things happened.

1) A stray cat delivered 5 kittens under our deck. We kept two of them.

2) Unbeknownst to us, our vet had a staff meeting at the restaurant where we and some friends gathered to celebrate Chico's life. As we were backing out of our parking spot, I looked into the window and saw our vet and his staff raising their glasses in honor of our little buddy.

Everyone loved Chico! Except, maybe his mother.
Terry & Lynne Wisner

"There are two big forces at work, external and internal. We have very little control over the external forces such as tornados, earthquakes, floods, disasters, illness and pain. What really matters is the internal force. How do I respond to those disasters? Over that I have complete control."

- Leo F. Buscaglia

Photo courtesy of kimobilevet.com

Chapter 5 - Having a Beloved Pet Euthanized

As a well-spent day brings happy sleep,
so a life well used brings happy death.

- Leonardo da Vinci

The word 'euthanasia' is translated to mean 'dying well". Most veterinarians consider this a peaceful, gentle death. It is more commonly referred to in the animal world as being 'put down' or 'put to sleep'. Accepting that the time has come for this option is one of the most difficult decisions a pet owner will have to make, yet, unfortunately, thousands face it every year.

As my friend Dee wrote when she knew I was doing this book;

Just a little more on having pets euthanized. Some pet owners will not stay with their pets when they have them put down. No matter how painful it is for a pet owner it is so very important to hold your pet as they go through the process of leaving this life. Even if your tears are blinding you your pet's love is showing in his eyes as he slowly leaves you. It is one of the saddest parts of being a pet owner.

Most vets give a poem called over Rainbow Bridge, where you will meet your friend when you die. You both will be strong and well and young and together. I have often wondered how I will be able to greet all of the animals of mine over the Rainbow Bridge."

Dee

Gwen and Kirby

I just had to have my little white Staff Yorkshire Bull Terrier named Guenivere euthanized at the beginning of May.

I found out she was sick when I took her to the vet after she stopped eating about mid-April.

That dog usually had a pretty hearty appetite, eating everything from apples to broccoli to chicken feet, so I knew something was terribly wrong.

The vet thought it was likely liver cancer. Due to the nature of the disease and the treatment, we decided to let things ride out on their own.

Her weight dropped dramatically in a few weeks, and then she collapsed and had a seizure. I had to make the decision.

I knew making the decision would be hard as she was the first dog that was my own and I had received her as a gift 13 years before from my brother Marc. Ironically, I am living with my brother, who is also a dog owner, and who had just been through this same thing two years ago.

I was able to talk with him throughout the whole situation. I decided to have a doctor come to my house and do the procedure there. I think this made a huge difference as I didn't have to worry about her spending her last minutes on a cold metal operating room table. I was able to cradle her head as she quietly passed. The vet then took the dog away for cremation, and then returned the ashes to me a few weeks later.

I don't think I have healed yet, but it's been important to talk to other people who have lost pets. People who don't have pets don't "get" it. Most say that they are sorry, but then don't really know what else to say. I've got a picture of her on top of her box of ashes. I keep a little note next to it that my eight year old niece wrote me that reads "Gweeny gweeny Gweenny Loves Loves Loves Loves You You You Uncle Monkey (my nickname). She drew a heart and a dog face at the bottom.

I've attached a picture of her playing with her kitty friend Kirby.

If you have any questions or want more details, just let me know.

Best Regards,

Michelle Sieling

Death is the ultimate measure of physical loss. How we respond to the physical death of a beloved pet resembles or symbolizes the way we respond to all major losses. It may be the “straw that breaks the camel's back” and we grieve not only the pet, but all the losses we have had previously and will have in the future.

Grieving heals us, even though the loss remains.

Neezie

The last pet I lost was the dog of my heart. From the time he was 9 years old he had chronic relapsing pancreatitis. He had an enlarged heart as he grew older, and mitral valve disease. A Yorkshire Terrier, he also had a collapsing trachea. And, lest I forget, irritable bowel syndrome. He was, to the AKC, Ch. Cap'n Ebenezer of Woodridge. But he was always my Neezie.

He was nearly 17 when I had no choice but to put him down. He told me it was time. I gave him the last gift I could -- release. I held him in my arms in a darkened room at my veterinarian's hospital. She gave us a few moments alone. And then she put him down while I held him. My heart shattered into so many pieces I doubt that I will ever find all of the shards. We communicated so well, the bond was so strong that it defies words.

I drove in pouring rain, through blinding tears, to bury him with his canine family in his breeder's Oriental Garden. He was buried with his beloved Pooh Bear who went everywhere with him. It was tucked under his arm for that final journey.

Warmly,
Darlene

Darlene Arden, CABC
Journalist/Author/Speaker
http://www.darlenearden.com
Author of *The Angell Memorial Animal Hospital Book of Wellness and Preventive Care for Dogs, Unbelievably Good Deals and Great Adventures That You Absolutely Can't Get Unless You're a Dog, Small Dogs, Big Hearts, and Rover, Get Off Her Leg!*

Euthanizing a pet can be very confusing for a young child. Do not use the words “put to sleep” or “went away in their sleep” as they may fear falling asleep. If you were concerned about the financial aspects of caring for the ill pet or having them euthanized, the child may misinterpret your words and think you would not take him to the doctor if he was sick.

Simply reassuring the child that he is safe and will always be cared for. You may choose to tell him or her that the doctor will give a painless injection of a powerful medication which allows the pet to die and not suffer. Make sure they know that this is not the same kind of a shot or vaccination they receive at the regular doctor’s office.

Tyson

Animals let their humans know when the time has come to let go. They will look at you with a look that tells you "it is enough." They want to reassure you that it is okay to let them go.

Tyson was 21 years old and had been with me since he was 4 weeks old. I had found him in the middle of the street in a mud puddle, 4th of July weekend, 1987.

I honestly did not think Tyson was going to make it to his 21st birthday, as he had been dealing with kidney and liver issues. But he did! We celebrated his birthday on July 4th, 2008.

But by July 21st he was very weak and was not able to walk unaided. We spent the night watching movies in bed. I hoped and thought he would die peacefully in his sleep. Not so.

The next morning there was Tyson up walking around wanting his favorite morning snacks, sliced chicken in gravy. While he was eating, I went to take a bath and he followed me in as he always did, to make sure I was doing it right.

He laid down on the towel by the tub and looked at me with those beautiful eyes as if to say, "it is time to say goodbye."

On July 22, 2008 we said our final goodbyes. It was so hard.

Michele Arthur

Rainbow Bridge

Just this side of heaven is a place called Rainbow Bridge. When an animal dies that has been especially close to someone here, that pet goes to Rainbow Bridge. There are meadows and hills for all of our special friends so they can run and play together. There is plenty of food, water and sunshine, and our friends are warm and comfortable.

All the animals who had been ill and old are restored to health and vigor. Those who were hurt or maimed are made whole and strong again, just as we remember them in our dreams of days and times gone by. The animals are happy and content, except for one small thing; they each miss someone very special to them, who had to be left behind.

They all run and play together, but the day comes when one suddenly stops and looks into the distance. His bright eyes are intent. His eager body quivers. Suddenly he begins to run from the group, flying over the green grass, his legs carrying him faster and faster.

You have been spotted, and when you and your special friend finally meet, you cling together in joyous reunion, never to be parted again. The happy kisses rain upon your face; your hands again caress the beloved head, and you look once more into the trusting eyes of your pet, so long gone from your life but never absent from your heart.

Then you cross Rainbow Bridge together....
Author unknown...

Submitted by, Ginny Brancato
Founder: http://www.rainbowbridge.com
Wishing you all the best! Sincerely,
Ginny

Now he has departed from this strange world a little ahead of me. That signifies nothing. For us believing physicists the distinction between past, present, and future is only a stubbornly persistent illusion.

- Albert Einstein

Photo courtesy of ifda.org

Chapter 6 - Grief is Natural

Only those who avoid love can avoid grief. The point is to learn from grief and remain vulnerable to love.

- John Brantner

Everyone has to deal with grief sometime, and most people work through it given time. If you find that you are trying to deal with a number of stress factors at the same time the loss of the pet may just become overwhelming.

Animals teach us and speak to us in the language of spirit and love. As humans, we learn to interpret their looks and non-verbal clues to know how to treat them when they are sick. Just as with beloved human friends, we may want to extend their stay longer than they do. They are eager to go to “their next great adventure” and know they will meet us on the rainbow bridge.

All life is filled with Hellos and Goodbyes. The longer we live there will be greater number of loses; of people, pets, things, ideas, jobs, seasons and so on. We must then learn to say a **good** goodbye. By allowing the sadness of loss to really be felt and experienced, we can then incorporate the lessons taught and joy received when we did have the gift and move on.

Four Things That Matter Most

My friend Ira Byock, M.D. an international leader in palliative care who wrote *The Four Things That Matter Most- a book about Living*, in addition to his remarkable book *DyingWell.* He reminds us to say the following four things that matter most:

- Please forgive me.
- I forgive you.
- Thank you.
- I love you.

And in working with those who are dying or have died we say the fifth thing that matters most and that is:

- Good bye

These simple statements are powerful tools for improving relationships, not only with the dying but with the living. One of the most important things we can learn from a relationship, whether it is with another human or an animal, is what it can teach us about ourselves.

When the student is ready, the teacher appears

What we learn from the other part of the relationship is what we need to know in order to move forward. The one who left you and you are grieving was your companion, friend, soul mate etc. But, most of all they were a teacher. Their lives interacted with yours, in order to teach you lessons you will need to know in order to be the kind of person you were meant to be.

Of course, we miss, mourn and grieve the passing of that teacher. But their lessons remain and hopefully we will not only have learned valuable insights into other relationships, but also about ourselves.

Molly

I received an email from a friend who is on a internet newsletter that brought this topic up. I was forwarded this because I lost my 11 year old yellow Labrador mix last year to cancer. I would like to share my experience with you, in which you are more than welcome to use for your story.

I was 12 when I got Molly, at the time I was working under the table at a pizza shop in Trenton, NJ. After work, I went to my mom's work, which was the Emergency Room. There a yellow lab mix stray came in causing chaos immediately in the waiting room. When security was about to take her away,

I approached her to allow her to notice me, and from there, fell to her back, showing belly. Covered in tar and pretty skinny, I told them that I would take her. The ride home consisted of "I can't believe you took that dog... your dad is going to kill you!," while Molly slept in my lap.

Molly grew up to be a great dog. I took her skiing, and swimming at various of places such as the oceans, local creeks, rivers, and lakes. Her neighbor, who was a golden retriever and her best friend in the canine world passed a few years back. So we decided to get her a new friend, a chocolate Labrador that we named Nellie.

They grew to be fantastic buddies, Nellie was her daughter. Molly though was starting to grow older, less active, and developed cancer, Nellie was not use to this so we got Nellie another play mate, Saranac, a black Labrador.

As Saranac grew to be the beast she is today, Molly's cancer worsened. She became lethargic, that night I took her to the emergency hospital where we euthanized her, her spleen burst, and there was a cancer tumor deep in her chest that was affecting her breathing.

Coping wasn't easy. Molly was my baby for 11 years, I put my life into her. Even neighbors had felt the loss. Nellie and Saranac helped me through by being loyal companions.

I decided the next day to send out an email telling all my friends.

For some reason or another my breeder that I got Saranac and Nellie from was on that email list, she told me about a yellow lab pup she had that was given up by her owners.

snatched her right then. Having 2 just wouldn't cut it! Chimay is the third. She helped get my mind off of things and onto other things. I thank my pups for getting me through the loss.

hope that's helpful for your story :)

Patrick

Looking at Grief Stages

There are very distinct, yet overlapping, phases of grief. We go through the stages in various orders and in varying degrees on the road to recovering from any loss. If we lose a jacket at the ballpark, we may go through all the stages in a few minutes. If the jacket was one that was given to us by our brother on our birthday, it may take much more time.

If the animal was a family pet and stayed outside, it may not hit us as hard as if he were our own companion and greeted us each night when we came in the door. If your pet was a companion and best friend, the mourning will be a deep one.

1. **Shock/Denial/Numbness.** We can not believe this has happened to us. Our body and emotions numb themselves against the pain. The mind denies the loss. Often we will say things like "This can't be true." One of the valid reasons for memorials and funerals is to acknowledge that death did take place. That our beloved will no longer be with us in body.

2. **Fear/Anger/Depression.** After the numbness wears off and we are once again able to feel, then all of our repressed feelings come roaring back. Sometimes these feeling are not rational at first and can seek someone to blame, either an outsider or ourselves. "I can't share how sad I am about my dog, because my co-workers will think I am crazy." "But, on the other hand, I inquire about their child's cold and buy their stupid Girl Scout cookies to support them. It isn't fair!" "Oh God, please don't let me start crying at work again. I heard someone call me a drama queen and say; It's only a dog, not a child." "I just need someone to acknowledge my sadness."

3. **Understanding/Acceptance/Moving on** We finally realize that the world will continue to turn, that loss is natural part of the cycle of life and that we will make a new and different existence without our loved one. Moving on does not mean forgetting the lessons we have learned from our loved one. We have the memories and experiences of good times as a foundation for the remainder of our lives.

4. **New Hurts may Trigger Old Wounds.** You may have denied yourself the right to go through these steps with an earlier pain. Perhaps you muffled your emotions with food, drugs, alcohol or sheer force of will. Now, that you are more open and your heart is raw and vulnerable, these areas of past loss may come forth and need to be healed. Give yourself the gift of healing and letting go of old pains and resentments that can keep you stuck.

Final Gift from Your Pet – An Open Heart

This is the final gift of love from your pet is an open and receptive heart. Many people try to soften their heart in meditation and prayer. But when you are grieving, your heart is already soft and vulnerable. Some say it is even raw.

This physical and emotional hurt has opened spaces in your soul. Grief has caused you to naturally be reflective about who and what you are. Now, in that vulnerable place, you have the opportunity to heal and grow in new ways.

Do other unresolved issues in your life need to be examined and explored? If so, this may be the time when your heart is open enough to hear the prompting of the spirit urging you to forgive yourself and others.

I want to ask you to look down at your body right now as you read these words. Are your shoulders hunched and your arms held close to your sides in a protective form? Are you guarding your heart by closing down around it?

Then, throw your shoulders back and breathe down deep into the center of your heart. Allow it to be open and wide and accepting. While you are breathing, think of the breath going side to side and open your heart even more so you will have a wide open heart. Stretch your arms out and feel the difference.

Jasmine

People who don't think of their pets as a part of their family do not understand the grief that comes with losing a pet. If you have lost a pet, do not feel ashamed to grieve…the grief is real.

If you know someone who has lost a pet, let them grieve. Don't tell them that it was just an animal and they can get another one. While most pet lovers will get another pet, it is not a replacement for the pet they lost. Luckily, we still have three other cats that we love for their own individual qualities, but there will never be another Jasmine.

Some of the nicest gestures were when we received sympathy cards from my sister's dogs, as well as from the vet who took care of Jasmine in her final hours, and others who didn't send cards but still understood my grief and cried with me.

If you would like to read more about Jasmine and my other pets, please visit:
http://MaureenGendron.com/petsblog.

Maureen Gendron
Maureen@MaureenGendron.com

Be Kind to Yourself

Show yourself the love and kindness your pet gave you. If you need to feel bad, then do so. If you need to cry, then cry. If you feel like laughing and dance, then laugh and dance.

Stay open to the still small voice inside you that is giving you permission to fully feel and allow the healing to take place. This grieving process can take as long as it needs to take for your heart to heal.

Always remember that your pet gave you unconditional love, a gift not easily replaced. It is right and natural that you would grieve their passing. You will truly miss them.

We understand death for the first time when he puts his hand upon one whom we love.

- Madame de Stael

We give dogs time we can spare, space we can spare and love we can spare. And in return, dogs give us their all. It's the best deal man has ever made.

- M. Acklam

Photo courtesy of pattersondogandcat.com

Chapter 7 - Expressing Our Pain

We had a dog, Apples. He was 13 years old, toothless, blind and had the worst breath this side of Jabba the Hut. But he was the sweetest dog, and I cried and cried when he died.

- Marlee Matlin

"There is no pain so great as the memory of joy in present grief."

- Aeschylus

Shock is a temporary escape from reality. As long as it is temporary, it is fine to be dazed and unbelieving for a time. However, if a person prefers to remain in this state rather than face the reality of his loss, it is unhealthy.

It is normal for a death of a beloved pet to raise questions about our own lives and mortality. If you find that the focus of your thoughts surrounds death you may want to talk to someone.

In many conversations with friends who have lost pets, who were more like children, they expressed the concern they had about embarrassing their friends and coworkers with their grief. One woman, who routinely brings casseroles to sick neighbors and is so supportive of community activities, but tried to deny her own needs for comfort. Why? Because in her mind, she was afraid that others would think her “silly” or that “it was only a dog,”

Pain from loss does not just go away because we deny it exists or that try to convince ourselves prematurely that we are “over it.” It has been long been known by medical doctors and psychologists that the more pain is denied, the deeper it tends to go inside our bodies and minds. The deeper that pain is hidden in our cells, the harder it is to identify and deal with. The deeper the pain is buried the more damage it can do to body, mind and spirit.

Killer

When I met and married the man of my dreams I had no idea I was going to fall in love with a five pound Yorkie named Killer. I had never had an animal in my life, so to have really hit the doggie lottery so to speak was amazing. Killer had such personality that everyone who knew him fell in love instantly, even people who did not like dogs.

He was very much his own little man. He had quite an amazing life as well, he traveled everywhere with my husband and me, was the Hallmark Christmas Tree Ornament twice, ate in some of the finest restaurants in the city, and was a model in almost all of my style shows. His fans were far and wide, many times when I would pass people I didn't know them, I would hear them whisper, "there goes Killer's Mom".

What a lot of people don't know was that after my husband passed away, this amazing little dog became my salvation. I had to get out of bed every morning and come home every night because he needed me. He comforted me like no one else could, he was such a part of my husband Tom that it made me feel good just to be with Killer. And so after fifteen years of a great life, Killer passed away very peacefully, on to what I hope is a great time with Tom now.

After he passed away I felt as though my whole family was gone and it was very difficult. So with my grief I have started a foundation in Killer's Memory. It is called ARKI (Animal Rescue in Killers Memory I), and we are trying to raise awareness about Breed Specific Adoptions. Many people don't know that if you don't find the breed you want to adopt at the shelters, that you can find many great people who take specific breeds into their homes and help rescue these dogs from Puppy Mills or families who can no longer care for the dog. So if someone wants a specific breed, yet still wants to adopt it is possible, you can go to Petfinder.com and find any breed you want.

Knowing that I could never replace Killer I resigned myself that I would never get another dog. However, when I was doing research for the foundation I came across a great group called "Little White Dog Rescue" in Omaha, Nebraska. They rescue Westies, but they had a tiny Yorkie who had been turned over to a kill shelter from a Puppy Mill raid. I sent off a quick note to the rescue and listed my Yorkie Credentials and within twenty minutes I had a phone call. The rest they say "was meant to be" and with that I was lucky enough to adopt the cutest little Yorkie who needed me desperately.

Tallia Tinkerbell Tierney has become the poster girl for our big event that is going to happen in September. We are doing a style show in Killer's memory and raising money for the dogs in the shelters who need warm coats in the winter and to help the shelters who take these dogs into their homes and spend their own money to get them well enough to be adopted.

One of the places I found comfort after Killer died was in a song, I have included the lyrics. It so touched my heart, it is by the rap star Babyface. I can't even tell you how hard it was to find this song on a CD, but all the folks at Barnes and Noble did not give up until we found the CD. I have practically worn it out. I played it the night I had Killer's memorial with a few friends over and announced the kick off of ARKI, my friends were more than generous, we raised $1200.00 dollars that evening, and we had not even asked for donations yet. What a tribute to little Killer. And everyone who met Tink wanted to know where they could adopt one just like her. Hopefully, something good will come out of this and educate people that even if they want a specific breed of dog, they can still adopt.

Anne Tierney
Director of Corporate Gifts
Halls Crown Center
200 East 25 Street
Kansas City, MO 64108
(816) 274-8200
Fax: (816) 274-8231

PK, My Cat

I travel a lot for my work. My vet told me my cat of 14 years, PK, had diabetes. This was the day before I had a class to teach in Washington, DC, which is a long way from my home in Phoenix. Ironically, I was teaching emotional intelligence to scientists of the Department of Veterinary Sciences. My vet said I should go. PK would be fine for a week without insulin. I could start when I returned.

The night before the class, my cat sitter called. PK seemed very sick so she rushed her to the vet. Thirty minutes later, the vet called to tell me PK had taken a turn for the worse. Something else was wrong. She explained what she had found. I was in such a panic, I couldn't hear her. In the end, we decided that exploratory surgery would not be worth the money. She didn't think PK would make it through the night.

I knew I had to say goodbye to her in spirit. When I went to bed, I called to her as I would do at home. She always slept with me when I was home, pressing her warm body next to mine. I imagined she was with me. Through my tears, I actually felt her there. It was as if her spirit came to me that night. We slept together for the last time.

That morning, the vet called to say that PK had miraculously made it through the night. She was still very sick but seemed peaceful. During lunch, I returned a call from the vet. PK had died mid-morning. I cried in the bathroom, then tried to breath myself back into looking sane. As I began to teach after lunch, I lost my voice. I had to stop. Fortunately, I felt a classroom of people dedicated to understanding the life and death of animals would understand. The class was very supportive. After taking a walk and looking at the sky, I could return and complete the class.

Yet I was still filled with guilt for leaving her. Whether valid or not, when I returned home I hired a pet psychic who told me, "PK is fine. She chose to leave while you were gone. She couldn't leave you while you were together." It might be a justification, but I felt it was true knowing how emotionally tied we were. And I knew that someday I would see her again.

I honor PK with a memoriam in my garden. It is a statue of an angel cat with wings sitting under three glass mushrooms. I smile when I see it. She still brings joy into my life.

Dr. Marcia Reynolds
http://www.Outsmartyourbrain.com

Pain Can Be Physical

Many people are surprised by how much grief and loss can hurt physically. The most common physical symptom is low energy and fatigue. You may need a lot of extra sleep. This is not just an escape, but allowing your heart to rest and your soul to rejuvenate.

Your body may not be as dependable as it once was. I have found grief to throw me off balance. I feel out of synch with the world going on around me. Others have told me they felt uncoordinated and clumsy.

After a loss, you may find your immune system is vulnerable and you may get sick more often. Be sure to take vitamins, drink water and try to eat a balanced diet during this time of emotional upheaval.

Emotional Symptoms

When you are grieving, your emotional life may be unstable and unpredictable. You may find yourself more moody, irritable, easy to take offense and self absorbed.

You may dwell on unrelated fears and fantasies or think of yourself as "on automatic pilot" or just "going through the motions."

Whatever emotional turmoil you are going through is normal and to be expected. Recognize that this is an opportunity for learning life's lessons. So be open and sensitive to the changes you are going through and do not fall into the shame and blame that so many people use when something bad happens in life.

Miki

Hi Judy,

Two years ago, my 19 1/2-year-old cat, Miki died. We found someone to come to our home and help her pass on. This woman was an angel and I have written a whole story about how Miki passed on and what a beautiful experience it was for my husband and I. [I can send this to you, although it's far too long--3 pages--for you to use.]

But I entered a state of depression. I had never before been depressed, so it was all new feelings I was dealing with. I couldn't stop crying. After about five days of crying, I decided to call my friend and acupuncturist, Renae. I asked her if acupuncture might be helpful. She worked me in right away. The relief was immediate. The depression started coming back about a week later, so I scheduled another acupuncture treatment. That was all I needed.

I still feel Miki's spirit whenever I think about her. We have her ashes and hope to one day scatter them on top of Mt. Oklahoma, an almost 14,000-foot peak here in Colorado, which is named after the state of Miki's birth.

I recommend acupuncture for anyone dealing with depression and loss.

Hope this is helpful to you.

With kindest regards,
Alyson

Alyson B. Stanfield
Website: http://www.artbizcoach.com
Blog: http://www.artbizblog.com
Book: http://www.idratherbeinthestudio.com
Twitter: http://twitter.com/abstanfield
Facebook: http://www.facebook.com/profile.php?id=725081176

P.O. Box 988, Golden, CO 80402, USA
303.273.5904, alyson@artbizcoach.com

Ultimately, the only way to get through adversity is to just put one foot in front of the other and keep walking. There really is no short cut on this journey back to wholeness. You can't go over the pain. You can't go under the pain. You can't go around it. It must be dealt with in order for you to heal. You simply must go through it. It will take as long as it needs to take.

Billy

Everyone who met Billy knew he was special. Not only was he an unusual breed (Platinum Burmese), but he acted like a person.

His cat mother had died when he was born, and he was hand fed by the breeder.

We're convinced he didn't know he was a cat.

We lost him to kidney disease, so we had about six months to resign ourselves to the loss. (It didn't help.) Probably the best thing I did was write a farewell letter to him. It took me a long time, as I cried so hard I couldn't see the computer screen. We buried the letter with him, along with a piece of red ribbon (his favorite toy) and some yarn from the afghan (his favorite blanket). His grave is in the backyard, marked by a wire cross.

For months I visited him every day, telling him how we missed him. We also went to three sessions with a grief counselor, read a book and listened to some tapes. But I think the letter, the somewhat ceremonial burial, and the support of friends were more helpful than any of the more professional services. (I got more sympathy cards for Billy than I had received for the deaths of my mother, father or brother.)

His picture is still on the mantle. We now have two rescue cats.
Billy would appreciate the fact that it took two cats to make up for him.

Kay Paumier
Fremont, CA
http://www.communicationsplus.net

Monroe

I've now lived through the day that began with Monroe, and ended with no Monroe. Monroe was a cat, belonging to me and my wife Jill. He was about 16. Most people in the world never met him. Most people never heard him chirp when they entered a room. Their loss. Mine, too. He's been gone for weeks. The tears have cooled. I no longer cry in the cat food aisle, where all good owners go to stare at the cans and say, "Nah, he don't like that one."

In that aisle tonight my only thought was for how I had to go home and, before I forgot, figure out how the world is different without him.
Because the world did change that Tuesday, right around lunchtime, when the vet uncurled her stethoscope, tucked one end under his black and white chin, and said, "He's gone."

Near the end he hardly ate. Not Fancy Feast, not bratwurst, not Fancy Feast and bratwurst mixed with milk. Day by day we'd watched our alternatives, and his future, evaporate. His rear legs had stopped working; the vet said it was part of kidney failure.

On the night before Monroe had been in bed with me and Jill. Beside her sleeping form, he and I stayed awake for a couple of hours, and I thanked him for the moments he'd had with me around. Thanked him for being a big tuxedo boy from Massachusetts, like me a New Englander among New Yorkers, although he was the better dressed.

I thanked him for all the times he played with a long handle of the spoon under the blanket. I thanked him for batting at a string in the air. Thanked him for eating like a Doberman, weighing 15 pounds and for enjoying his life. Much as a New Englander can.

Thanked him for all the days and nights, and all the chirps. I wished him well, while my wife slept. The next day we watched him on the couch, his back to us, his nose to the cushions. Too soon we carried him down in the elevator, while somehow the business of our apartment building continued. In the elevator we ran into a cat owner. "Awwww, poor kitty," she said. She knew. Monroe knew. My tears came up by themselves.

Jeff Stimpson
http://www.jeffslife.net
Speaker to educators, parents, and professionals
Podcasts at jillandjeff.podbean.com
Author of *"Alex: The Fathering of a Preemie"*

Remember, sadness is not depression. Depression is a general state with no focus and sadness is very much focused. You know why you are sad. “I am sad because my cat died.” “I am sad because I miss my pet very much.” “I am sad because this brings back all the unresolved conflict with my mother.”

If your sadness is intense or you feel that life is becoming overwhelming, perhaps you need to visit with a counselor. I have heard good reports about Cognitive Behavior Therapy, which is short term and action based and doesn’t have you tell your story over and over and over. Our daughter Debra, who is an energy worker, also recommends EFT (see below) as an effective method of releasing pain and getting out of “stuck” places.

Samantha

Hi Judy,

On April 15, 2008 my cat passed away. I adopted her when she was 4 and she was 13 when she died. I think you will be interested in my story, especially with what helped me to heal from it and even cope with it at the time.

My cat Samantha began to vomit her food. She couldn't hold anything down. This caused her to stop eating all together. I was frequently at the vet, who was confused. I finally had to keep her home and feed her with a syringe and use an IV to give her fluids. Although she was sick she didn't seem like she was suffering emotionally and I decided I wanted her to pass away at home.

In the morning of April 15 I woke up because I felt her moving. She opened her eyes, meowed, began to shake and just like that I saw her pass away. I was looking at her the moment her soul left her body. It was a shocking experience and if I didn't know EFT I'm sure it would still be a haunting memory.

Emotional Freedom Technique (EFT) is a technique that combines ancient acupuncture points with modern psychology. When you are feeling stressed you use your fingers to tap on different acupuncture points. If this is the first time you have ever heard of EFT I strongly suggest you look into it. It's a technique that is sweeping the nation because it is so effective.

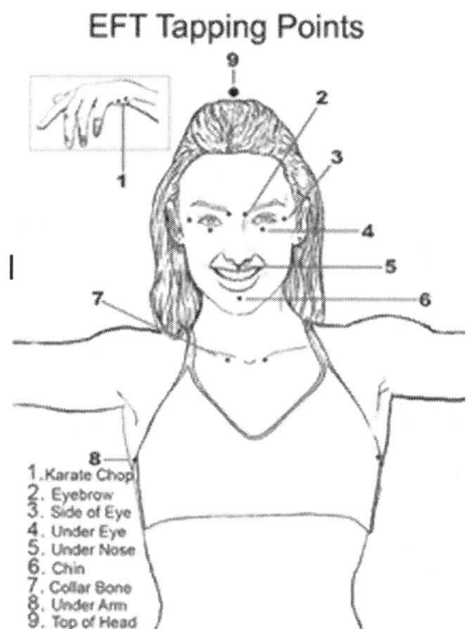

I had produced a documentary about EFT and Samantha first became sick the week before my premier. I had a massive workload and my cat was dying. I don't think I would have been able to get through it without EFT.

While using EFT you say what is bothering you while you tap on the meridian points. It is such an incredible emotional release. I began to use EFT while she was dying. One night I was so exhausted and emotional distraught that I just began to cry and then I took a deep breath in and focused on all my feeling while I was tapping. It was a God sent.

I am attaching a picture of the meridian points. The website of my film is http://www.TryItOnEverything.com. You can get instruction on exactly how EFT works

To honor her memory I made a stepping-stone with her name on it and placed it in the woods where she is buried. Instead of feeling traumatized from seeing her pass away I now feel blessed that I was able to be by her side.

If you are sincerely looking for ways to help people grief over the death of a pet then EFT is something you should look into. I made a movie about it so of course I am biased but I am so grateful I knew this technique when she died and I hope others can find to same peace that EFT helped me find.

Wishing you the best,

Jessica

Harley

Judy,

I would be happy to share our family's story about our dog Harley. We've had other pets over the years....but Harley was special.

How we were told: We were told by our vet, "There is nothing more we can do for his lung condition. He may live for some time, but you will know if you feel it's time to allow him to move past his suffering." Like most families caring for a loved one, we did everything possible. Daily pills, sprays, powders, calm environment, etc. and as a result, we enjoyed him and he enjoyed us for another nine months. The decision to help him end his suffering was intense and emotional. We made appointments, cancelled appointment, looked into alternative medicines and finally decided his quality of life was reduced to a few good moments each day rather than good days amongst a few bad. My husband is a very strong man and I have only seen him breakdown on a few occasions. This was one of them.

How others reacted to your grief: Harley was an idol in our neighborhood. Never having a fenced yard, he lied under our massive willow tree and guarded our property line in a way that represented a "proud owner and keeper" of his land.

Everyone loved him and they comforted us we prepare for the decision and provided great emotional support afterwards. There were many questions from the smaller children in the neighborhood who could understand where "Harley" went.

Even know when we see those children, they reconfirm that Harley is in doggy heaven.

What helped you heal: It was toughest for my husband, who lost a pet when he was very young and his parents basically "discarded" the animal and significance – they were farmers. Anytime he brings it up, we just talk about the good things, talk about how we saved Harley from the pound and gave his nine years of a wonderful life with a family who loved him. Also reassurance from family and friends that our decision was right.

How we honor his memory: Pictures, I now use his picture as my bookmarker for daily devotions, and keeping his ashes in a special hand-carved wooden box. Although this summer we are going to have a small ceremony and put his ashes under the willow tree so he can forever protect our home.

I don't have a picture here at the office, but will bring one in and send it to you.

Neat project and thank you for letting us share our story.

- Colleen and the Rudio Family (Jeff, Zach and Jordan)

Everyone Has Suffered Some Loss

In my work with grieving families, it appears that those who manage to keep fairly busy and continue to carry on as many of the usual activities as possible during a crisis, adapt better and heal faster.

Well meaning friends and family may want to coddle or take over as a way to show concern. You may long to climb in bed and stay there. If you think about the past when surgery patients were kept in bed and told not to do anything after the trauma, you will remember that it actually took them longer to heal. When I was born, my mother was in the hospital for 10 days. When I had children, I stayed for 2 days and then went home to resume activities. I think our daughters use drive in windows they are in and out so fast.

You need some time to heal, physically, emotionally and spiritually, but you heal faster with movement. Your heart and mind can still process the emotions but some activity will assist by getting your cells to release the pain.

Emotions provide a blueprint and motivation for everything we do and feel. We should not apologize to others for how we are feeling. Nor should we assume that no one understands the pain we are in.

It is true, that each incident is individual and so no one has grieved exactly like we do, but they still empathize and understand on some level. Every single person alive has suffered some kind of loss. The feelings of being alone, sad, depressed or blue are universal and normal in everyone at one time or another in life.

If you are feeling despair after the loss of a pet, recognize that it is to be expected. For some these feelings of pain will move quickly. For others, it may take additional time to process the emotions and move toward healing.

Keep moving. You will make it. I have confidence in you.

"Given the choice between the experience of pain and nothing,
I would choose pain"

- William Faulkner

Photo courtesy of yelp.com/biz/monterey-bay-lovedpet-royal-oaks

Chapter 8 - Guilt and Regret

"When one door closes, another opens; but we often look so long and so regretfully upon the closed door that we do not see the one which has opened for us."

- Alexander Graham Bell

As mere mortals, we will be saying goodbye for the rest of our lifetime. We will lose jobs, friends, pets, car keys, houses, our abilities and finally our life. A primary feeling that accompanies loss is guilt-regret.

Many assume that guilt-regret it is one word with one description "I'm a rotten person. If only, why didn't I, I shoulda, coulda, woulda."

There is a distinction between the words and understanding and that difference can make it easier to overcome the negative connotations and process the authentic emotions.

Guilt is a deed that has been done for which you are sorry.

For example, in the following story by Kathleen, she is over come with guilt for allowing Thumper to stay outside while she was gone for a short while.

What occurred was an accident, an oversight, an unfortunate turn of events. What happened to Thumper has happened many other times with children, family, neighbors etc. It was no one's fault. It was an accident that could have happened to anyone. It was not a deliberate act of unkindness, but an isolated incident that had a sad ending, but could just as easily have been completely unremarkable and ordinary.

Kathleen happens to be a friend and one of the kindest, most companionate and thoughtful people in the world. Her guilt is misplaced and certainly mitigated by the thousands of considerate acts she has done in life.

She needs to forgive herself. The animals already have.

Regret is something you wished you would've done, but did not

For example, wishing you had said "I love you" more often or played ball when you knew that your dog wanted to go out and romp in the yard with you.

The problem with guilt-regret being lumped into one word or negative emotion is that they feed on each other. When regret is lumped with guilt, it makes the guilt last much longer and gives it a power and size in our hearts and minds that is harder to process and let go.

Feelings of guilt and regret can be so overwhelming that they become deep, dark secrets and mind chatter to be shared with no one. They grow in our thoughts until they become beliefs and actions. (See my book and course called *Building Self Confidence With Encouraging Words* available at http://www.EncourageSelfConfidence.com for additional information.)

When I am working with children on this area I recognize they don't have the verbal ability to form into words some of their feelings and so I watch their body language for clues. When approached with the nonjudgmental; "We all do things we are sorry for later. Let's talk about something that has happened that you now wish you had done differently."

I can see their relief in finding out that it is okay to make mistakes or poor decisions as long as we learn from them. Brooding and constantly thinking of the "bad" things we have done does not give us the freedom to remember all the "good" decisions we have made.

Some People Feel Guilty for Grieving a Pet

Since I announced to friends and relatives, I was doing this book, a number have commented on the guilt they felt for grieving or showing emotions in the workplace. Many have told me that they have been called "Drama Queen" or worse when they tried to process grief in the workplace.

A woman approached me privately to share the following story:

Tangles, My big Loveable Mess

Hi Judy:

Tangles was a big, hairy, slobbery, stinking mess of a dog and I adored him and he idolized me. No matter how often I bathed and brushed him, he always looked and smelled like he had been riding the rails for months. He was hit by a car recently and I was devastated and in shock.

I called in to say that I needed some time off when Tangles died, my boss said "Gimmee a Break. He was a freaking dog. It's not like he was a real child or anything."

So I used up my personal days crying and looking for another job. Unfortunately, I have not found one yet, so must disguise both my name and that of my beloved pet. At work and in public, I am careful not to overstep what is considered polite conversation and keep my emotions hidden in my heart.

Society is not ready to accept that to some of us, our pets are our children. And no one would suggest to someone that lost a son or daughter, "Well, why don't you just get another one. Only this time get one that is small and well behaved."

This relationship was one of the strongest I had ever had. The real irony of this is that my confidant and best friend was my dog. Now, I have no one I feel comfortable sharing innermost feelings with.

Thank you for listening.

Anonymous

Regret and guilt are not productive emotions. You don't need to feel guilty for what has happened or how you feel. These are just realities.

Thumper, Prissy, & Dixie

I once had a beautiful Siamese boy named Thumper. I was going through a divorce and had moved into an apt. We had only lived there about a week and it was Mothers Day 1980. Thumper was outside and wanted to come in I said, "no you can play outside a little while longer and when I went to go to dinner with my parents I couldn't find him. I reluctantly left for dinner and when I returned I found him dead in the driveway. He looked like he was sleeping but he was gone. I took him to my parents and buried him under my favorite tree. To this day I cannot forgive myself for not letting him in when he asked. It brings me to tears this day over 28 years later. I have never forgiven myself.

For twenty three years I shared my life with the sweetest little girl named Prissy. All of her life she appeared to be about six months old because she was so tiny. She shared all the good and the bad of those twenty three years. On the night of July 6, 2003 she had a seizure. I could not reach my vet so took her to a 24 hour emergency vet and he said if she were his he would put her to sleep. It was 2am and about 100 degrees out and I was all-alone and did not want her to suffer so I made the choice to end her life. I held her in my arms while she passed from this world. I later came to realize that she was probably dehydrated from the heat and would have been fine if the Dr. had given her subcutaneous fluids. Another decision I regret. I had her cremated and she is buried in my flowerbed with a statue of a cat with wings and her name on a plaque and a miniature rose that is as sweet and beautiful as she was.

I do not know if I believe in reincarnation but I adopted a feral cat that was born approximately the time Prissy died and she is the image of Prissy. She is sweet and kind and small like Prissy and has a comma next to her nose just like Prissy had. I think God sent Kiarra to me to help ease the pain of my loss.

In March of 2007 I was cat sitting for my best friend. She had gone to New Orleans for a wedding. I stopped to feed Dixie on my way to work and found her dead in the cat box.

She was still warm and I probably should have tried to revive her but was so distraught that I didn't even think of it. I removed her from the box and cleaned all the litter off of her, brushed her and wrapped her in her blanket. I had loved her as my own and could not stop crying because I knew I had to call Judy and tell her what happened. I had called my work to tell them I would be late but I could not stop crying so they told me to take the day off. I had just suffered a personal loss and dealt with that fairly well but finding Dixie gone brought all the emotions I had bottled up flowing out of me.

I know that all of my animals are waiting for me on the rainbow bridge and I know that I will see them again. I could not survive without their unconditional love and comfort. It is wonderful to walk in my home and see their little faces waiting for me. They make my house a home.

- Kathleen Springer

Temporary feelings of regret are a normal part of the mourning process. This helps us retrieve our lost dreams. If we hold on to regret, we risk trapping ourselves in a prison of unrealized dreams from which it is difficult to escape.

- Barbara De Angelis

Photo courtesy of awakeparent.com

Chapter 9 - Pet Loss and Children

If you have a dog, you will most likely outlive it; to get a dog is to open yourself to profound joy and, prospectively, to equally profound sadness.

- Marjorie Garber

The loss of a beloved pet may be the first death experience children face. It is very traumatic for the child and should not be trivialized. Their feeling and emotions are very real and they are trying to process the situation as best they can. They need the support and understanding of caring adults to work through what has happened and what it means to them personally.

Pet loss and the surrounding activity can be a catalyst for growth and understanding with the whole family. Talking and sharing thoughts and emotions is one of the best ways to cope. That is why people gather after a funeral to share stories and acknowledge the part the deceased has had in their lives.

It is a teaching moment to share openly about what is going on in our hearts, minds and bodies. Recognize that not all children or adults grieve the same way. So, do not expect the child to be openly sad or to be appearing uncaring in their attitude about the death of their pet. It may take some time to process what this loss means to them.

No matter how the child may appear to be taking the news, do have a period of time just for them to talk and you to listen. After sharing their fears or concerns, you will want to reassure them that they are safe and loved. This may be the opportunity to teach the values and beliefs that you may not have shared with your family.

A great many of the people who deal with depression or feelings of suicide as adults suffer from some sort of sorrow they never had the opportunity to work out as a child.

Helping the Child Process Emotions

Guilt, regret and sadness can be such powerful feelings, that the child may forget all the pleasant interactions that took place with the pet. When you can help them to shift the focus from bad to good, you assist them to lessening the power of guilt.

Here is a list of activities to do with the child to help them heal from loss:

- Make a list of good things you did together
- Draw a picture of the pet.
- Use modeling clay to make a figurine.

- Save a small amount of fur in an envelope.
- Write a letter to the deceased.
- Send a card to others who are sad about the loss.
- Release a balloon.

Many times a child will feel a deep responsibility or guilt that “if only…..” they may think that it is their fault for not remembering to give the pet food or water, or that they left the door open, or they had mean thoughts about the pet. Because children do not have enough life experience to think in the abstract, all of the problems faced by the family in their mind, stems from their own actions or because of them.

Sandy, one of the many contributors, wanted to share this sweet story:

The Meaning of Life

Being a veterinarian, I had been called to examine a ten-year-old Irish Wolfhound named Belker. The dog's Owners, Ron, his wife, Lisa, and their little boy, Shane, were all very attached to Belker and they were hoping for a miracle.

I examined Belker and found he was dying of cancer. I told the family. We couldn't do anything for Belker, and offered to perform the euthanasia procedure for the old dog in their home. As we made arrangements, Ron and Lisa told me they thought it would be good for the four year old Shane to observe the procedure. They felt as though Shane might learn something from the experience.

The next day, I felt the familiar catch in my throat as Belker's family surrounded him. Shane seemed so calm, petting the old dog for the last time, that I wondered if he understood what was going on. Within a few minutes, Belker slipped peacefully away. The little boy seemed to accept Belker's transition without any difficulty or confusion. We sat together for a while after Belker's death, wondering aloud about the sad fact that animal lives are shorter than human lives.

Shane, who had been listening quietly, piped up, "I know why." Startled, we all turned to him. What came out of his mouth next stunned me. I'd never heard a more comforting explanation. He said, "People are born so that they can learn how to live a good life - like loving everybody all the time and being nice, right?"

The four year old continued, "Well, dogs already know how to do that, so they don't have to stay as long."

Author Unknown

Sharing the experience opens the door to a respectful communication with caring adults on the emotions surrounding this death and others the child will experience in the journey of life.

As a parent educator and family relationship coach, I always recommend telling children the truth as much as possible, while being kind and aware of what they need to know at the time. Here is a story from Sarah, a cousin, who found out as an adult what had actually happened to a beloved pet.

Sweet Alfalfa Breath

could hear his whinnying from the truck before I could even see his slick bay-colored coat running for the gate. My Uncle Sid and I were on our way to visit Nugget in the pasture, just outside Helena, Montana. As Uncle Sid and I drove down the dirt road towards the pasture, Nugget lifted his head and watched our dust cloud approach the barbed wire fence. I was only five at the time was not big enough to get the gate open.

I remember Uncle Sid opening the gate while trying to keep Nugget in. Nugget would get so excited to have company; he would prance about and whinny. Then I would get so excited to be within petting distance of a horse, I would prance around waiting for Uncle Sid to get the gates open.

Nugget was a registered Appaloosa horse, though I never really understood why because Nugget was all one color, a bay (which means brown with black mane and tail.) His mane was very full and beautiful but he had a short ratty tail. He had a glistening, short, brown coat that seemed to change color the more you brushed him. I loved to brush him.

The best part of Nugget to me was his nose! In case you didn't know, a horse's nose is very soft and sensitive with little wiry whiskers that give feedback to the horse and scrunch up when you have overstayed your welcome prodding around their fuzzy nostrils. I loved to rub Nugget's nose on my face and give him kisses, while breathing in his sweet alfalfa breath.

As the years past I moved away with my mom, and Uncle Sid sold the property where Nugget lived. My cousin Brandy, Sid's son, was given the horse. Tragically one evening Nugget spooked and caught himself in the barbwire fence. Nugget's leg was injured beyond repair and when Brandy found him the decision was made, that the injury would be impossible to heal.

Nugget was sold.

As a sensitive little girl, my mother forbade Brandy to tell me what had happened to Nugget. I was told that a very nice family with young children, like me, had adopted Nugget and would ride him lightly and allow him to live the rest of his life in their pasture.

When I was 19 years old, I had the opportunity to move in with Brandy and his wife for some time. One evening while reminiscing over dinner about my beloved Nugget, I asked Brandy who had bought him and if I could visit him.

Brandy agreed that while I was too young and sensitive to handle the truth then, I was a mature adult and could handle it now. He admitted that Nugget had not gone to a family, but rather to a man in Helena who would trailer sick or injured horses to Canada for the meat market in Europe.

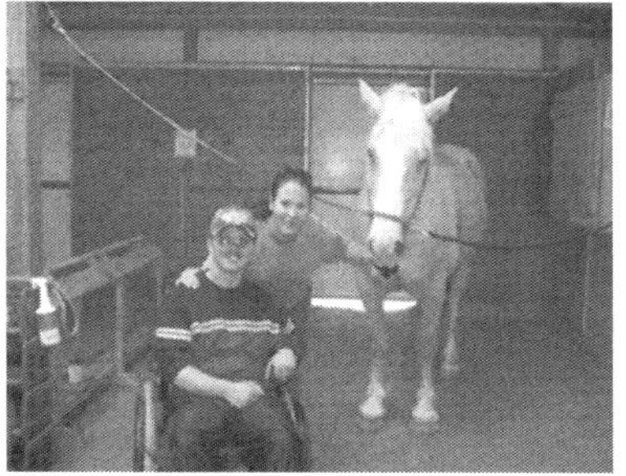

have never been as devastated by old news as I was that evening sitting at the table listening to the story of Nugget's unworthy end. I literally felt my heart break.

have unforgettable memories of Nugget, and visiting him in the valley. His life was well worth living, short as it may have been, for giving a little girl the ability to fly, smell sweet alfalfa breath and nurture a love of horses.

Sarah Elizabeth Smith
http://www.whitehorsehealing.com

P.S. This experience and the connection I felt working with horses has directed my career choices. I am now getting a masters degree in social work, specializing in equine facilitated mental health and education services. I've been spending my summers working with physically and emotionally challenged people using horses for therapy.

There is nothing better for the inside of a person than the outside of a horse.

- Will Rogers

Pets Teach About Life and Death

Children can learn the importance of responsibility at an early age by acting as a caretaker for a pet, but may feel the reason the dog was killed by a car was because they weren't responsible enough. As a caring adult, you will want to allow the child to feel the sadness and then help them to recognize that accidents happen and there is no reason to feel shame or blame.

It is important that they recognize that the life span of a pet is somewhat shorter (usually) than a human and so they aren't expected to live as long. When the fish dies after a month, we acknowledge the happiness we enjoyed together, even as we flush the remains down the toilet. Children need to be taught that all life is precious, but some may be shorter than others

Pets can also help children learn to deal with medical illness as they take part in the care of a sick and helpless animal. This is a prime time to teach about caring and compassion.

By the time we reach our teenage years, many of us have grown up with our pets, and they're part of the family. Just like losing a family member, when a pet dies it has an impact on those who cared for him or her.

Children who grow up in a house where all life is respected may react to the loss of a pet in a great variety of ways. Accepting death and being free to talk about feelings and emotions is a beautiful gift that kind, loving parents give their children.

If they have been able to participate in the activities surrounding the loss, they will be better prepared in life when they face other inevitable deaths of friends and loved ones.

Many adults have told me that one of the reasons they were so traumatized by the death of a pet or loved ones, was because of the taboo that surrounded acknowledging death when they were a child. When they saw their parents stoically showing no emotion over disappointments when they were a child, they interpret that to mean that if they do feel sorrow deeply as an adult, they have failed.

Here is a story from Melissa, a sweet granddaughter who is 8 years old:

Melissa and Peter

It was one little puppy I really liked. He was my favorite and his name was Peter. He got a sickness where he could not see, eat or go to the bathroom. So we took him to the vet and she said he was going to die, just like Patches, his brother had done.

We were all sad and crying and the vet said just love it till it died. My Mom was watching a movie while holding Peter in her lap on Mother's Day. She fell asleep just rubbing his back and when she woke up he was dead.

Then we decided it that we would bury him in a box that she had gotten her mother's day gift in. We all decided it was just the right size for his coffin. We wrote his name on it and Amanda, my big sister, put him gently in the box.

We dug a hole outside and put the box inside and put a stick with his name on it. We were going to hold a ceremony, which is what we usually do when an animal dies, but Amanda got a phone call while looking for a song, so we just said a little prayer and that was that.

On Memorial Day, we made a bouquet of flowers and took it out to his grave. Can you believe it, he died on Mother's Day and we finally got around to having the ceremony on Memorial Day!

I think when a child loses a pet, the whole family should be sad with them. I liked it that I did not have to be sad alone.

My Dog Skip

The dog of your boyhood teaches you a great deal about friendship, and love, and death: Old Skip was my brother.

They had buried him under our elm tree, they said — yet this wasn't totally true.

For he really lay buried in my heart.

- Willie Morris

Tarbaby and Marcia

My first cat was Tarbaby, a solid black cat who ran into our house in fear of his life. Of course I wanted to keep him, so my mother cleaned him up and eventually he became a large part of our household. He lived for fifteen years.

I was still a child, and his death was one of my first experiences with the passing of a loved friend. Tarbaby had become old, and didn't move as fast as he once did. One day while returning from a shopping trip, my mother didn't see him and hit him with our old 50 Plymouth. He didn't at first seem hurt as he went to his favorite sleeping place, but unfortunately he was mortally injured.

It was my mother who had to tell me what she had done when I returned from school. I hated my mother for at least the rest of the day, but even as a child, knew that nothing could return my friend to me. Mother was sorry and knew how I felt. She was understanding and compassionate.

My aunt and cousins were also understanding which seemed unusual as they were farmers who knew of the loss of pet animals. My teacher at school insisted I write a tribute to my cat, draw him as I remembered him, and bury the paper with him. I did that, as well as put up a wooden cross to mark the spot in the back yard.

I still go there to look, though the cross has disappeared long ago. I still remember.

Marcia Dumler
Perry, KS

Pets Teach Responsibility

Most families start out pet ownership by their children with a fish. Whether it is a fish, turtle, cat, dog, goat, rabbit or hamster, caring for another living thing will do much to teach your child about assuming personal responsibility.

They also learn many values and life lessons about kindness, patience, reading non verbal clues as well as anticipating the needs of another. By connecting with an animal, it frequently gives a child the ability to then show that unconditional love to others.

Sarah Smith, who has a story included in this anthology, works with youngsters and horses, and has seen amazing transformations of attitudes and self esteem that come with interaction between children and animals.

I want to close this chapter with an article I wrote some time ago about explaining death to children. Perhaps it will help you.

Explaining Death to Children

© Judy H. Wright, Parent Educator

"Why did Grandpa go away? Was he mad at me?" "What happens when you die?" "Is Grandma going to cry like that forever?" "Can I go play now?"

When there has been an unexpected death of a loved one, adults often fail to realize that children can be confused by adult reactions. The emotional reactions by different members of a family may range from crying and hysteria to laughing. Children will know that something is wrong, but may not have the life experience to put snatches of information into the context of their thinking process. Children may also imagine that something has happened that will threaten their safety and security.

Provide Age Appropriate Information

Many people in Western cultures are uncomfortable using the words: dead, death or dying. Instead, the event is described using euphuisms: passing over, passed away, and transitioned to the other side even gone to sleep and won't wake up. Children, who may have seen bugs die, or dead birds, or may even have buried a pet, really have no frame of reference for "passing away."

Children need to be given information about the death, in a caring and calm manner, according to their age and understanding. Each child will then be able to absorb the reality and begin grieving and processing facts and feelings in his or her own way. Putting this information into a context he or she can understand will generate questions. This will give you the opportunity to clear up any misunderstanding and validate the child's feelings.

Take the Time to Explain

Children want to please the adults in their lives and watch for verbal and non-verbal clues to what will make the adults happy. If children sense their questions are annoying or upsetting, they will stop asking questions. Take the time to answer the questions and explain that each person grieves and misses a loved one differently. There is no right or wrong way. Encourage them to talk with others who are involved. Such conversations may even include sharing stories of happier times.

If it is your belief that Grandpa has gone to Heaven, explain how and why to the child. In our family, we used the analogy of the glove with the hand removed, to illustrate the spirit leaving the body. We then explain what happens to the body (glove) after the spirit or soul is separated.

Older children tend to be more interested in the actual process of death. They want reassurance that death is not usually so unexpected and that we, as parents, are not going to die soon. The younger ones are not sure whether they should be having fun with their cousins while the adults are crying.

Allow them to Say Goodbye

When is the right age to allow children to attend services? It depends on the temperament, age and maturity of the child as well as family expectations. Whether a child attends the actual funeral is a mutual decision made after a caring adult explains what will happen, who will be there, and what to expect. If the child was close to the deceased, he or she should be allowed to take some part in commemorating that person's life, perhaps by planting a tree or writing a letter.

Death is a part of life, but a child's first experience with losing someone can imprint how he or she will handle deaths and disappointments in the future. It is important to reassure children that they are loved and safe. Explain also that love and support does not end with physical life and memories of Grandpa will enrich a person forever. What was your experience as a child with death? How did you explain death to a child?

In his grief over the loss of a dog, a little boy stands for the first time on tiptoe, peering into the rueful morrow of manhood.

After this most inconsolable of sorrows there is nothing life can do to him that he will not be able somehow to bear.

- James Thurber

Prayer on Losing your Dog

Creative force, creating still,
Thank you for my beloved ________.
In a world of uncertainty, her love was constant.
She entertained me and kept me company.
Her brief little life was a gift that
Enriched and deepened my own.
But pets are companions only
For a portion of our journeys.
And now she is gone,
Leaving a hole in my heart,
An empty spot on my couch.
No wagging tail greets me
And no one wriggles with delight as I return home.
I have known her always by
Her sweet devoted presence and joyful playfulness.
From now on, I will love her in her absence.
There may be other dogs to keep me company in life.
There will never be another ________.
For ________, O Gracious Wisdom,
I am truly grateful.

Prayer Instructions:

Often we spend more time with our pets than with any of our human friends. When they die our grief can be overwhelming. Mourning their pets may be the first way children encounter death. No matter how many we have, this pet will always have a special place in our hearts. Why not teach your children that ritual can ease our sorrow?

1. Make an altar or shrine (a box or a table-top altar) with reminders of your pet. Light the lamp and read the prayer.

2. Make a list of all the sweet things you loved about your pet.

3. On a separate sheet, make a list of everything she no longer has to suffer.

4. Make a list of the help you received if she was sick or hurt. If you received help during her illness, you may want to write thank you notes instead. (This may be a good way for a child to come to terms with what happened.)

5. Read the first list aloud and put it on the altar. Read the second list and burn it. Read and burn the third list. If your children are old enough, let them make their own lists and read them aloud. When you've finished with the other lists, read the first list again and put it in the box to keep with her things.

Prayer Essentials:

A Lamp or Candle   Matches

river prayers

Chapter 10 - Pet Loss and the Elderly

"Great golden comma of a cat,
You spring to catch my robe's one dangling thread,
And somehow land entangled in my heart."

- Lida Broadhurst

In my work with Hospice and the Quality at Life's End Institute as part of the Montana StoryKeepers, I have witnessed the love affair many elderly have with their pets. Pets force them to get up each morning, to get exercise, to focus on something outside of their own problems and a wonderful companion.

It is no wonder, so many who need hospitalization or assisted living refuse to go for help, for fear of leaving their pet. I have heard of people who are ill, but who downplay their illness to the doctor rather than take a chance of being separated from their pet.

There is a wonderful project called the Eden Alternative incorporating pets into the Nursing Home experience. *Life Worth Living: How Someone You Love Can Still Enjoy Life in a Nursing Home. The Eden Alternative in Action*. Let us hope that this trend expands as the Baby Boomers want to keep their pets with them.

Marley

On June 9, 2008 my little Pug, Marley just didn't wake up. He was a sensational being with an amazing personality. He was a big dog in a little body and very much a clown. A couple of years ago I changed my lifestyle completely taking on two jobs so I gave Mr. Marley to my Mom, a retiree, who had all day to dote on his every move. She cared for him like he was her grandchild spoiling him rotten. All the neighbors in her retirement community loved him too. He was a love and everyone loved him.

On June 9th I woke up at 4am to take my friend from Poughkeepsie NY to Newark airport to catch his flight. At around 7am my sister called from Massachusetts. We were using the phone as a GPS to find the airport so I didn't answer. Shortly after that, she called again and I knew something was wrong. I texted her back letting her know I would call her in a minute. I was thinking that it might be my mother or my father who are well over 75 years old and anything can happen. I waited until we were parked to call my sister back.

She gave it to me straight. "Marley is dead, Heidi." My reaction? I squealed and cried out his name and started to fall over. I had two friends with me luckily, my dear Partner, Wayne, and my good friend Jeremy. They both knew the dog really well and how much I loved him so they made a Heidi sandwich, each hugging me from the side.

I had my sister and brother-in-law put Marley in the freezer until I could make it Massachusetts. I made it there that day. I called Angel View Pet Cemetery, in Middleborough, MA, www.angelview.com and made arrangements for a cremation for $145. Angel View is amazing and I recommend their services to anyone. Sitting on the bench by their coy pond with my boy's ashes and thinking about all the joy he blessed my life with was helpful.

Another thing that helped was seeing his little body in his resting position like he went to sleep so peacefully. I pet his soft little head and took a couple of pictures of him resting. It sure beat having to bring him to the vet suffering. I am thankful it didn't come to that. He also lived a great life and that makes me happy.

I decided I would skydive his ashes with a bunch of my skydiver friends. I am a skydiver and he spent a lot of time on the ground when I was jumping. Since my partner and I are in the video production business,

I will video the event and make a short video tribute to Marley calling it MARELY'S FIRST JUMP. Part of his remains will stay with Mom, part will go in my garden, and some in a piece of jewelry. I also put up a picture of him in his Halloween costume as an angel at work and put his year of birth and his year of death on it. People call me with their sympathy, or tell me they are sorry. It helps.

Useful resources... friends and family who love animals, the poem Rainbow Bridge, other poetry about losing a pet.

Pablo Neruda also wrote a very amazing poem about losing his dog that was raw and helped me to cry out a lot of my grief. I think my heart aches most when I think of the void his passing left my Mom with.

I hope this helps. Please contact me if you need any more information.

Sincerely,

Heidi K. Eklund
Poughkeepsie, NY

Djermag

Djermag came into our lives in 1991 and left us at 6:55 a.m. on the 8th of December, 2000. She died in peace.

She lived a good life...our "little terror" who raced across the carpet as if possessed, launched off the grand piano onto the living room drapes. Like the comics, except this was for real, she "shredded" our sheers and tore the drapes as she valiantly clawed to the top and then along the drapery rods from where she leaped to the ledge.

Once on the ledge, she loved looking out the round window above our front door. We sometimes called her "White Bite" because she bit the hand that fed her, especially if the hand petted her along her back and tail. She also hated to be brushed and despised showers. But once she was clean, she licked all her fur in place and walked on her tippy-paws like royalty.

In October we took her to the Skilled Nursing Facility where my father lives. Fearful, she buried her head in the blanket like an ostrich. But Djermag was popular, everybody loved her. "Oh, she's so pretty," they said. She shared her life with us for 10 years. We found her walking along the fence in our back yard. We weren't sure if the squeaky noise was a cat or a rat! This animal looked so mangled, mangy, etc. David offered her some food...in her excitement she fell on the wrong side of the fence and was gone!

She turned up a short while later and ate a third of a large can of food. David set out more. She ate that too. She polished off 3/4 of a large can of cat food! We stopped feeding her because she looked so bloated!

After two weeks of feeding her, she was gaining weight. We decided to keep her. David washed her. By the time we took her to the vet she weighed over 6 pounds, still about 40% less than the normal weight for a full-grown cat.

Over the days, weeks, and months her behavior led us to believe she had been abused. We asked the vet to remove a BB from her left leg, only after we had the ear mite problem cleared up.

We treated her with patience, kindness, and a lot of love. She was one fortunate kitty! Our friends rarely understood our patience with her given all the ruin she left in her wake. But she was our baby. Our BIG baby! She ate and ate and ate! Reaching over 10 pounds, she became the largest of our three babies.

Over the last month we noticed her getting lighter. Two weeks ago she was on the roof of our house. David laughs in amazement when a raven swooped too close and Djermag reached up and swatted the bird. Yet during the last few weeks she had more trouble holding food down. She lost 25% of her body weight and eventually stopped eating and drinking.

Despite repeated visits to the vet and being seen by specialists, the last morning of her life she threw up blood from the lymphoblastic cancer that had infested her stomach.

Our poor baby, our "little terror," our "fighter" fought enough. Despite her efforts she could not win this battle. She had the bad kind of cancer, the kind that would not respond to chemo (which we learned has an 80% success rate for cats). No, her time was up.

So sadly, we took her bundled in soft blankets in her little bed early morning on December 8th, 2000 to the emergency clinic. As David held her forelegs and I held her head and repeated her name, the vet injected her in the leg. Her eyes told me everything...

"I am at peace now."

© 2000 Brenda Avadian, Djermag's Mom

For many elderly people, like our next-door neighbor, the pet is their sole companion. They live alone and do not have a strong support system. They read friend's obituaries daily and worry that they will be next. The pets may represent independence and security for them.

The pet becomes a focus for their affection, attention and routine. The pet listens to the stories over and over again, never tiring or complaining. The love of a pet, especially to an housebound person, is unconditional and the companionship priceless.

Should the animal become ill, profound guilt may come into play. Often on fixed income and with little savings, they may be hesitant to pay for expensive treatments or visits to the veterinarian. They may even be sharing their 'meals on wheels' with the animal, rather than buying food specifically designed for their pet.

Should the animal die, those who are elderly are faced with even more difficult decisions. Housing restrictions, transportation or mobility problems and their own expected life span may contribute to the decision to not get another pet. And if they do decide to replace the old pet, the new addition may not fit in the environment or require training the owner is unable to do.

The death of a beloved animal to an older person can be very traumatic, as it brings up emotional issues of other losses in life.

Animals who Outlive their Owners

Under ideal circumstances, a family member or close friend will step as guardian for your pet should something happen to you. However, if you have not made those instructions clear to caregivers and family members, the pet may be euthanized or given to someone you would not have chosen.

You may want to set up a trust for your pet. Trusts can stipulate all the details an owner finds important including favorite foods, veterinarian, schedules etc.

The Human Society offers a free fact sheet on estate planning. There is also a website where you can download a simple trust according to the laws of your state. See the resources for Peace of Mind Pet Trust.

Use the same care in choosing a guardian for your pet as you would a guardian for your child. You will want the transition from your love and care to someone else to not be an additional trauma for the pet who is left.

Miss. Margaret and I

The origin of this story can not be counted on as being totally factual as the event took place over a half century ago, and as we age sometimes what we remember as being true may in reality have only been a dream.

What I can recall is, my mother enjoyed visiting some of the elderly ladies in the neighborhood and she'd take me along with her. One lady she'd visit was Miss. Margaret, an overweight woman who had hair that looked dirty grey; she spoke with a rather piercing voice that I recalled to be as annoying as her squawking green parrot.

I didn't like going to Miss Margaret's place. I wanted to play with the cat next door instead. Then one day my wish came true as my mother and I never went to see the old woman again.

I asked my mother, "Why weren't we going to Miss. Margaret's house?" She said, "Miss. Margaret has gone home."

A few years later I understood what my mother meant: Miss Margaret had died, and I wondered, what was on the bird's mind as to what happened to his pet.

Rosien-Margaret: Miss Margaret and I

Miss Margaret and I shared the same little apartment for a number of years, and I know that I would have felt lost and forlorn if it wasn't for her.

Miss Margaret was wonderful to have around, but I would have loved to have other company to share a meal with, but no one ever came to the apartment and the only ones I'd ever see would just fly by the apartment window, sometimes looking in, but it was as if I didn't exist. I felt so lonely, and then I'd hear her singing and I'd thank God for Miss. Margaret.

I'll never forget her sweet voice as she sang to me through the bars of the gilded cage. Though I never understood a word she was saying, I could still feel her love coming to me from her heart.

One morning as she was squawking, she fell and didn't move. As I saw her lying there, I knew that she had died and all I could do was cry.

Shortly after that, strangers came and took Miss Margaret away, and as I was about to be carried away, the stranger put the cover over my gilded cage. I cried out as loud as I could, but my cries went unheeded.

We all mourn at the loss of a loved one, even our pets. The way my cat Lewis is showing affection to me, I ask; do pets mourn at the loss of us?

J. T. Rosien
Anaconda, MT

It is a terrible thing for an old woman to outlive her dogs.

- Tennessee Williams

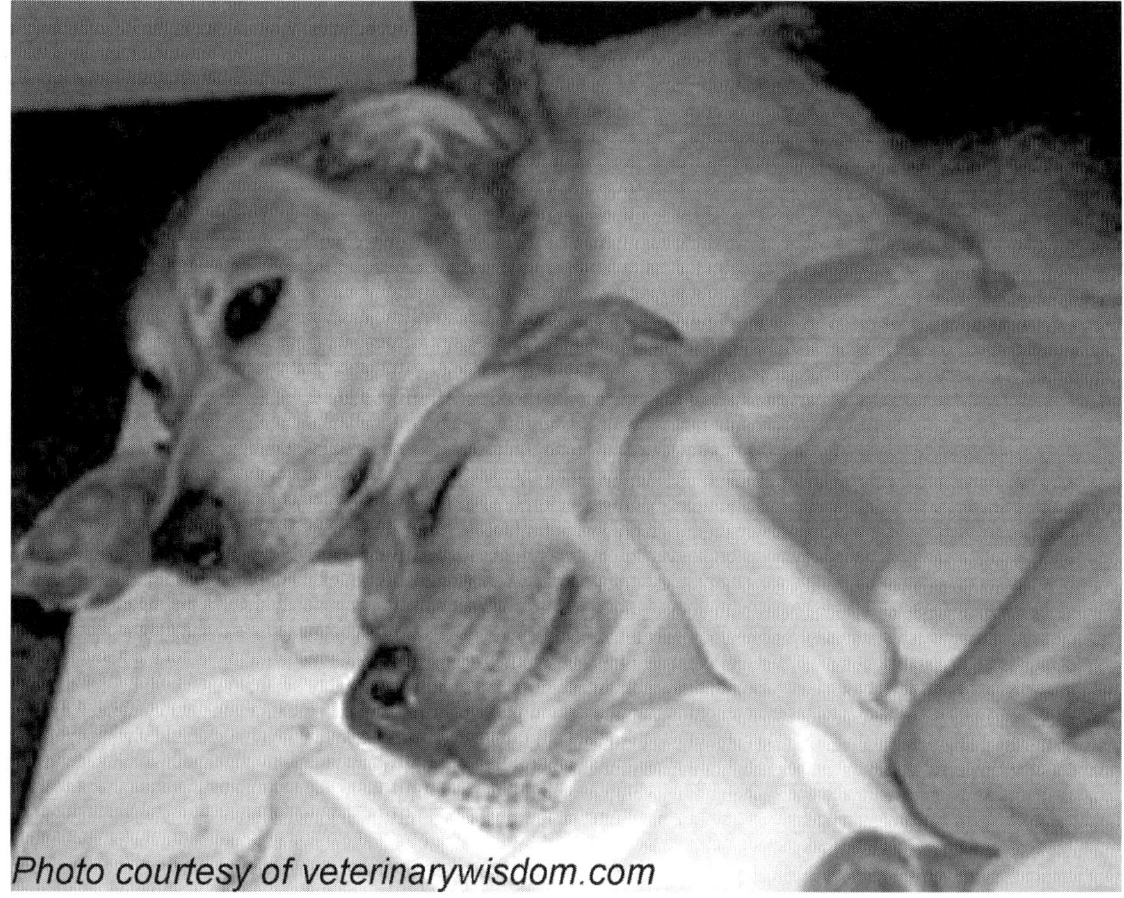
Photo courtesy of veterinarywisdom.com

Chapter 11 - Do Animals Grieve when a Companion Dies?

Dogs love their friends and bite their enemies, quite unlike people, who are incapable of pure love and always have to mix love and hate.

- Sigmund Freud

Many people have heard the remarkable example of devotion involving a Skye terrier dog who worked for a Scottish shepherd named Old Jock. In 1858, the day after Jock was buried (with almost nobody present to mourn him except his shaggy dog) in the churchyard at Greyfriars Abbey in Edinburgh, Bobby was found sleeping on his master's grave, where he continued to sleep every night for fourteen years.

- Jeffrey Moussaieff Masson

Do animals grieve when a companion dies? The simple answer is yes. The complicated answer is that they cannot communicate in words, so we must interpret their feelings by how they act and behave.

If animals can express fear, happiness and anger, why would they not feel sadness and confusion over where their buddy is? They may be looking all over for their best friend and miss the companionship of the games and relationship.

Miracle

Hi Judy, I saw your post in the MDMC Yahoo Group and decided to share a bit about our cat Miracle, who died last summer. Hope it isn't too long...

Miracle was always a very happy-go-lucky kitty who was affectionate and playful. He was a stray who we had found when he was only about eight weeks old. He grew up with our other cat, Nosho, who he teased with brotherly affection. He always had lots of energy until last summer, when we noticed him panting and generally being lethargic. At first we just thought it was the heat. It was especially hot in New York City last summer and we have no air conditioning. But we became very concerned when he began to eat very little (he always ate very well) and the panting continued after a break in the heat wave.

When we took him to the vet, we found out he had a congenital heart condition and that there was very little we could do for him. While we were discussing our options with the vet, he went into cardiac arrest and died in the vet's office. We were terribly heartbroken! It still hurts when I remember the veterinary technician taking us in to see him one last time.

We carried his lifeless body home from the vet's office in his carrier and made arrangements to bury him in my mother in law's garden. We created a marker for him and had a little service to say goodbye.

But back home, we both kept seeing him out of the corner of our eyes. It just felt like he was still with us. Our other cat, Nosho, missed him terribly and cried for several nights after he was gone.

Interestingly, though, after a time of grieving, Nosho seemed to change into more of an outgoing kitty than she had ever been when Miracle was around. Miracle was really the dominant kitty in the household and although we tried to give both cats equal amounts of love and attention, she had always been somewhat shy and never seemed to want much affection. This has changed dramatically over the last year. It just seems like Miracle's passing gave her the opportunity to be more of who she wanted to be all along, only Miracle's big personality was too much to compete with.

Although we miss him terribly, we still feel like Miracle is with us. We often talk about him and laugh about his funny ways. We also feel like he helped Nosho to be more of a cat than she was before Miracle came into our lives. He has truly left his mark on all of our hearts. We still feel he is very much a part of our family and always will be.

Thank you for asking, Judy!

Warm regards,

Sandra Winter
Sound Counsel
Transformational Coaching
Sound Healing
http://coachingwithsound.com
"Empowering You to Sing the Song of Your Heart"

Ever consider what our dogs must think of us? I mean, here we come back from a grocery store with the most amazing haul -- chicken, pork, half a cow. They must think we're the greatest hunters on earth!

- Anne Tyler

Watch for Non-Verbal Clues

Animals become very attached to their master and may become very stressed when separated. Because our animals have no verbal skills, they cannot tell us how they feel or what they are thinking. As humans, it is our job to read their non verbal communication clues and interpret what they need.

Pets may exhibit many of the same symptoms of their human counterparts.
If we notice they are more aloof or clingy, sleep more or less, or constantly go to the favorite place of their companion, we need to recognize this as signs of suffering and grief.

Just as we would offer sympathy and support to a human friend, we should also help them to move through the grieving process.

Elizabeth and the Dog Who Understood

When our black Lab-mix Riley died, I felt like our daughter Elizabeth died all over again. He was Elizabeth's couch companion for the last five years of her life, and after she died, he was never the same.

Elizabeth was born severely disabled as a result of me catching the #1 birth defects virus, cytomegalovirus (CMV), when I was pregnant with her. She couldn't walk or talk, so she needed friends who could understand her. Riley became such a companion.

When Elizabeth was 11, I called the animal shelter and told them I had a handicapped child and needed an older dog who would lie on the couch all day next to her. I was told, "We not only have a couch potato here, he's the whole sack!"

Riley was estimated to be about five when we brought him home. He performed as advertised, keeping Elizabeth company on the couch for hours at a time, always being careful not to step on her. He often greeted her with a friendly lick, making her smile. When she died at the age of 16 during a seizure, Riley rarely jumped on the couch anymore and preferred to keep to himself. One day he couldn't jump at all. We discovered he had tumors all along his intestines so we had him put down. We scattered his ashes around Elizabeth's grave so they could forever keep each other company.

I am managing my grief by writing a book about Elizabeth and Riley's "lump on the couch" relationship in hopes of encouraging others to consider older or trained dogs for their disabled loved ones and to teach the public how to protect their unborn from CMV.

Please visit my Web site at http://www.authorlisasaunders.com

Lisa Saunders

P.S. The attached photo is of Riley and my "healthy" daughter Jackie.

Johnny Weismiller, Famous Swimmer

My husband and I were building a log home while the building was going on we lived in a trailer on the property. Our cat Khaki-Wacky gave birth to 3 kittens under the trailer. The dogs bothered her so very much that she moved the kittens across the creek that ran through our property. The spring runoff came all of a sudden and two of the kittens were swept away.

From our trailer we heard this very loud mewing. We ran outside and saw this little golden fur ball crying wanting to cross the stream. The stream was a raging torrent, we called out "Swim Johnny, Swim." After much coaching this crazy little kitten jumped and Johnny Weismiller came into our lives. He lived happily as an outside cat and became somewhat wild upon maturity.

When I sold the house I wanted to take him with me. My son-in-law Brian climbed a large pine tree and captured him. He had a huge hole in his side and the Vet did not think he would live, but he did for 21 years. He outlasted Salty and when I got Duffy Do they were best friends. The death of this courageous cat was a period of grief for Duffy and me.

Animals do grieve for their loss of companions and Duffy was not an exception. He went into a deep decline. This caused me to rethink my promise not to have any more animals. But of course, I couldn't resist. So meet Fozzy Bear, who was Duffy's friend for four years.

Dee

What Are They Feeling?

My friend, Keek Mensing, who is an animal communicator and author of *The Way I Hear Them* says that animals not only miss their companions but will continue to communicate with them after one has passed on. She suggests we talk to our pets in complete sentences as we did when they were alive and sharing our lives and then listen with our hearts. She also suggests that we be very aware of our dreams. Pets who have died will frequently come to you in a dream, giving you reassurance that they are alive, well and happy in the next plane of existence

Tucker and Willy

Hi Judy

have waited while to reply to your email.

We had to put Tucker and Willy to sleep. They were 161/2 and 17 years old. Their photos are on our website.

It's funny how their health declined so quickly.

Tucker could hardly walk and his joints hurt so much he would lick them raw.

Willy just sat by the food dish. We had to drag him outside to do his business. He lived to eat. In the end he could barely do that.

Our vet was so wonderful. She and her assistant came to the house and first put them to sleep so they would be comfortable.

Then they just went to sleep with their noses touching. Bill dug a grave and they are buried together under a pile of rocks in the field.

Seth, our other lab had as hard a time as we did. He was not here, but knew something was missing. He would all of a sudden start to cry. I guess it was more of a howl.

He helped us thru the loss. He is number one now and is loving it.

It's funny how our dogs were like losing a child. It will take awhile to not feel their presence at home.

The picture of them really shows their personalities. Tucker outgoing and Wiily so shy.

Love, Judi

Judi Rivers
Broker / Owner

Animals are not only our good friends and companions, but are part of the wonderful world of nature. They have skills and talents that they share with others. Perhaps they may not be able to “talk” to us, but surely they “communicate” with one another and with us, if we listen with our hearts.

Of course, they grieve the loss of a companion, either animal or human. Their communication is often more of a “commune” or sharing of intentions that does not require mere verbal words.

This soldier, I realized, must have had friends at home and in his regiment; yet he lay there deserted by all except his dog. I looked on, unmoved, at battles which decided the future of nations. Tearless, I had given orders which brought death to thousands. Yet here I was stirred, profoundly stirred, stirred to tears.

And by what? By the grief of one dog.

- Napoleon Bonaparte on finding a dog beside the body of his dead master, licking his face and howling, on a moonlit field after a battle.

Napoleon was haunted by this scene until his own death.

Photo courtesy of southcentralkymonuments.com

Chapter 12 - Memorials, Tributes and Rituals to Remember

"...he will be our friend for always and always and always."

-Rudyard Kipling

Chip and Jessie

Carol's Memorials

On shelves in my living room, amidst the books I have read or should read, sit four wooden boxes with brass plates bearing the names of three dogs and one cat who have shared my life and passed away. The boxes, which hold the ashes of my past pets, are of different sizes. A small one for Mickey, my first cat. Two slightly larger boxes accommodate what remains of Dustin, a cocker spaniel, and Chip, a Pembroke Welsh corgi. The largest box belongs to Jessie, a 125-pound Bernese Mountain Dog.

(Chip is the Pembroke Welsh Corgi that died in January 2007. The other is a photo of the painting that was done of Jessie, the Bernese Mountain Dog, who died in January 1990)

Each pet brought so much happiness and great memories but also the heartache of losing them. I am fortunate to have family, friends and my longtime veterinarian who understand my attachment to my pets and have provided support on these occasions. Some of the ways they have shown this parallel the Jewish customs of mourning for people – the Shiva. They have included my family coming over to sit and talk to me and share stories about the pet as well as bringing over homemade meals. We all need an opportunity to "vent" our grief to an audience – be it one or many – which understands that our loss is real and profound. I often try to provide these opportunities for friends who suffer similar losses.

Probably my most profound loss was my first dog – the one that I grew up with and was part of our family from the time I was nine until he died while I was in college. Kelly was a handsome and sweet German shepherd dog. My mother was unable to tell me of his passing on the phone and sent me the sad news by letter. I immediately called her and we cried to each other on the phone.

He was truly a member of the family and we were all heartbroken. He was beloved by many in our neighborhood and we were pretty much identified as Kelly's family. He has been dead 35 years but we still talk about him, share stories about him. As we like to say, the Myth of Kelly grows with each year and each re-telling of his feats.

My most recent loss was in January 2008 when my corgi could no longer battle lymphoma which was diagnosed only a few weeks earlier. Efforts at chemotherapy failed to stem the disease. While he is dearly missed, at the end of March I added a new member to the family, a border terrier I've named Scooter who has already made great friends with the two senior pets in the home – two cats. I always find that "puppy fever" is a great balm to help heal the loss.

Regards

Carol Hodes
Old Bridge, New Jersey

Rituals and the Funeral Experience

Rituals, memorials and ceremonies to mark the death of a loved one are important. Some sort of a meaningful tribute, however small, will aid in the social, emotional and spiritual healing after a death.

This "closing ceremony" can be a song sung in your heart, a cup of tea raised in salute or a full-blown funeral with invited guests and speakers.

A funeral or gathering provides an appropriate setting that permits you and others to share stories and express feelings. It memorializes the role that the lost one played in the life of others and helps you to affirm the love and life you shared.

Checkers

Hi Judy,

Here is my story:

I had a cat named Checkers. She was a calico cat that I found as a stray kitten. I took her in. She was an indoor and outdoor cat. When I moved out at the age of 25 (which I believe was in 1994), she went with me to my first apartment. She became an indoor cat since I lived on the 2nd floor. She really became my companion and I always looked forward to coming home each day. She was just like me too. She was always independent. She would allow me to pick her up when I walked in the door but that was it.

She passed away in 2002, shortly after I started my MBA program. One day she was not walking right and couldn't seem to make it into the litter box. I took her to the vet. They weren't quite sure what was wrong. After a couple of tests and a $1000 later, it was determined she had a heart problem. It seemed that the blood was not flowing to her paws. It would require an operation that would cost another $5000.

I didn't know what to do and I didn't have that kind of money sitting around. They said to give her some baby aspirin to thin her blood but it was only a temporary solution. This went on for a couple of months and then things started to get worst and I knew I couldn't allow her to suffer. I called the vet and scheduled an appointment to have her put down. I was devastated to have to do it, but I stayed with her until she was gone. My roommate at the time was there in the waiting room, but there was nothing she could do to help me through this. I went home and cried. I missed her and she was gone. It was like my heart had been ripped out. I did the best I could and went on with life but each day I missed seeing her as I walked into the door. The vet sent me a card of condolence.

Even as I write this, it is so difficult because you never forget the moment she passed away. If this were a written letter, you would see my tears that were shed. I still have pictures of her and there are times I wish she were here to help me when things just don't go right in my life. Sometimes I use her name when I sign up for newsletters and such. It is a way for me to remember her always.

Thanks.
Antoinette Morales

Wakko

My dearest of my three cats, Wakko, died in May. In late April, he suddenly became very still and quiet. We took him to the vet. The vet noted the Wakko was dehydrated and let us know the next day that he had acute renal failure with only about 10% or his kidney functioning. I was devastated when my husband told me (he had talked to the vet). I could barely talk to the vet as the cat was so dear to me. We had raised him from 2 weeks old (his mother was one of our cats) and he was within a few feet away from me all the time.

He stayed at the vet for 10 days and we tried many different treatments. He seemed to be more lively when we were near him and after we knew there weren't treatments to help him, we brought him home to keep him comfortable for as long as we could.

He died the next evening, quietly, at home. Earlier that day he had looked at us with his deep look of love that was so characteristic. He had stayed near us all day. That was such a gift he had given us near the end. But, even so, I was devastated. I cried for days.

It sounds strange but to memorialize him I wrote an entry for my business blog (which is about needlepoint) and the first item in it is a needlepoint I'm working on because it looks like him.

HTH, I'm also happy to answer any questions you might have for me.

Keep Stitching,

Janet M. Perry
http://www.napaneedlepoint.com
http://www.nuts-about-needlepoint.com – blog

Conan

Conan, a large black lab mix had my heart. As he aged I wondered what I would do without him. The artist in me felt compelled to create sketches, watercolors and photographs of him. There was a strong bond between the two of us. I stayed awake for three days trying to nurse him through surgery, an IV hanging from my dishwasher, as he lay on his ugly orange rug. My husband said every time I spoke he could see the fight come into his eyes.

I wish I would have known then to tell him it was alright to go. Since then I make sure I give permission to my animals, letting them know I'll be o.k.

After his death I found myself in the art studio frantically creating a sculpture. The scene, Conan, in his usual position, I on the rug next to him cradling his back. We were almost the same size. I cried as I created this work of art. My husband came in and asked what I was doing, and if it was so painful why would I do it? I just sobbed, "Because I have to."

That sculpture was the first sculpture that I created in memory of a pet.

Soon after I was commissioned to create a sculpture of two children on a swing. I heard their dog was old and not expected to live, I included it in the sculpture at no cost. Conan died about 18 years ago. As an artist I specialize in creating memorials for loved ones, they are not just of the humans, but they are also of the furry friends that we love and cherished, and it started with the love for Conan.

Within my adult life I have had the honor and privilege of being a friend to quite a few animals. There were usually two dogs living in our household at any one time. As you can imagine, a few have passed on. I have an unusual tradition I started with my first dogs passing. When Conan passed I pulled out my sewing shears and snipped off a bit of his fur, wrapped the end in scotch tape and gently placed it in a ring box on top of a piece of his ugly orange rug. I would take it out from time to time and rub his hair on my chin or against my hand and think of him. My daughter was 5 years old when Conan passed, today she is 23 and has moved away. Our most recent family pet died of cancer. And when my daughter was told she asked, "mom did you save some of his fur for me?"

Bridgette Mongeon

E.T. the Turtle

One time my husband Ray brought the family a surprise gift when he returned from a business trip out of town. An associate had a turtle that they could no longer keep and so Ray volunteered to bring it home to our three young sons and me, all of whom are animal lovers.

The turtle was about 8 inches long and when he extended his graceful neck, he reminded us of a movie star, so we named him E.T.

Even though we knew a lot about animals in general, we did not know the specifics of turtle care. We went to a wonderful vet Dr. Sara Stephens, who was just starting her business and had a turtle in her office! Her turtle was 6 or 8 times the size of E.T. and very healthy. She told us she had gotten her turtle as a small child from the dime store. It had grown from about an inch and a half to it's current size.

She gave us supplements and instructions on feeding E.T. We force-fed him for a while before Ray and I had a weeklong trip planned and was leaving the boys and pets with a caregiver.

When we returned, E.T. had died. I was devastated! I literally howled with grief. My remorse and grief was much worse than with any of the other close family pets that we had lost in the past.

I believe my sadness was so deep because I felt that we had taken on a privilege and honor of caring for a life. For whatever reason that life was cut short. We had made the commitment to protect this animal and this charge should not be taken lightly.

E.T. went into the pet grave at the back of our garden. Through the years we have buried rabbits, cats, dogs and fish that have been loved and cared for by our family, as well as birds and squirrels. On the top of the pet grave is a huge Rhododendron plant that reminds us of our commitment to love and protect those animals who have been put into our lives.

Susie Risho
http://www.MontanaStoryKeepers.com

We do, indeed, have a stewardship over those who are vulnerable. However, there is a cycle of life and each one of us will face our own mortality as well as that of our loved ones. The best memorial to remember that love never dies. Building on the foundation of kindness, understanding and tolerance we have gained from pets, we can influence the world by sharing the message.

"A pet is never truly forgotten until it is no longer remembered."

- Lacie Petitto

Photo courtesy of petsandparasites.org

Chapter 13 - Do Animals Have Souls?

"No heaven will not ever Heaven be. Unless my cats are there to welcome me."

- Anonymous

"Until one has loved an animal, a part of one's soul remains unawakened."

- Anatole France

Two days ago we waded through the mud out to this grave beneath the pines at the foot of the hill to place a Christmas wreath on it, hoping he would look down from the Paradise of Ten Billion Trees and Unrationable Dog Biscuits and pity us.

- Eugene O'Neill, speaking about Blemie

You may or may not agree with my belief in life after death and the ongoing possibility of spirit-to-spirit sharing. I have spent too much time at the transition of loved ones coming into this realm of existence (birth) and leaving (death) not to acknowledge spirits, angels, heavenly beings or whatever they are called.

If you do, then I encourage you to recognize that physical death is not the end of the relationship, but just a continuation of love and caring. If you do not believe in an after life, that is okay too. Just enjoy every day to the fullest.

Trust Yourself

Pets who departed their bodies taught me years ago that there is no such thing as death. My pets always come back to visit me after they "die." They check to make sure I'm okay without them. They let me know they're thriving. If you're a pet lover, it won't surprise you to know that our furry friends are caring and compassionate even after they're gone. My eyes are filled with tears as I write this because my pets are always available to me.

Just as each dog or cat has a unique personality style and habits when they're in a body, they make their presence known after death in an authentic way. One dear departed soul pawed at the front door in her very distinct way, creating the "Mandy" scratching sound. She wanted to make sure I knew it was really her so she could comfort me. Of course, there was no physical presence at the door when I excitedly answered, but Mandy had made her point.

A beagle mix dog who had been famous for overeating swirled her energy around her food bowl in a secretive pattern until I joyfully acknowledged her presence. A cat who had already gone into rigor mortis by the time I discovered her body nurtured me when I was crying. She made her cold paw alive with warmth and movement until she had clearly communicated, "Don't you get it? There is no death!" My grief immediately ceased.

I'm not saying I don't still mourn the loss of a pet at first. I miss their physical presence. I long to hold their warm body close to my heart. Each furry best friend had a very special smell and feeling that I wasn't ready to release into the ethers. However, I understand the cycle of life and death because of my pets. Hospice work with a 16-year old hound while she departed her Earthly life in a state of euphoria helped me prepare for my own death. The vet had said, "She's in no pain. You are. Just comfort her as she completes her life span." I couldn't imagine life without "Sugar."

My suite-mate and I carried our baby in and out of the house during her last few weeks so she could relieve herself while she shifted between her old and new worlds. Eventually, Sugar became so comfortable in her new existence that she departed for good. On the way out, she gave us many final gifts, including taking us with her energetically as she explored the bliss of life after death.

Sharing the energy of Sugar's transition made me temporarily crave death because I discovered the beauty of The Other Side. It wasn't yet time for me to leave, so I eventually re-entered my daily life with passion to be more fully who I am while I'm here.

Just between you and me, dead people aren't strangers to me. When a friend recently lost her husband, Gary, he couldn't get through to her with certain messages he desperately wanted to communicate so he conversed with me. I immediately called my friend with Gary's loving disclosures.

My friend was greatly relieved, even though she still grieved the loss of her best buddy. As with other experiences with Souls on The Other Side, I felt very honored and privileged that Gary chose to communicate through me. His energy was clear, uplifting, and beautiful. His love for his wife was evident.

I hope this helps you if you are challenged with the loss of a beloved pet. I encourage you to be open to a new way of relating to your loved one. Departed pets, friends, and family members have become some of my most trusted Guides. Trust unexplained feelings, sounds, and events. I'd love to hear from you if I may be of assistance.

by Doris Helge, Ph.D.
http://www.TransformingPainIntoPower.com
http://www.MoreJoyOnTheJob.com

Animal Soul: Ode to Camper

© 2008 Ann Keeler Evans, M.Div.

People ask me: "Oh, you're a minister, what do you think - do animals have a soul?" I have to tell you, I don't really think about it like that. Here's what I know.

I've had a lot of loss in my life, many of them devastating. But none were more devastating than the losses of my sister's two children. Chad committed suicide at the age of 19. His sister, Jan, who was older by 6 years, died falling asleep at the wheel, after too many drinks, just a month shy of our family's fifth tragic anniversary.

One on top of another, the blows were crushing. I did my best to support my sister and her husband, my parents and the rest of us. I did both of their funerals — oh, so hard, so hard, so hard.

The summer after Jan's death, I retreated to the couch with a stack of mystery books. I was living that summer with my good friend Jenn. Jenn had two fabulous dogs, Camper and Boojum. Boojum is a little dumpster dog recovered and rehabilitated. She's friendly and happy and an all around great dog.

Camper was an aristocrat: a papered German Short-hair. I don't know if you've ever lived with a short hair, but they're high maintenance. They need a job all the time. They worry prodigiously – "what's going on, Mom, what do I have to do next?" Even Jenn had to admit he whined a lot. Camper was pretty clearly a one-woman dog. He loved each of us who loved Jenn, but he knew he loved Jenn best. He loved her better than anyone in the whole world could love her, although he admitted that Scott did a pretty good job of loving her.

So, if Jenn were in the room it was hard to get Camper's attention. That made it twice as wonderful when he appointed himself my companion and savior.

It was not a nice summer. Everything in my body broke down, trying to soothe my heart and mind. I needed extensive dentistry, I had poison ivy that wouldn't quit and I, on the cusp of becoming a woman of a certain age, was having female problems. I logged an amazing amount of couch time.

In fact the other amazing thing about that summer was that I wrote my first book and created and performed more weddings than in any summer before or since. So I was working. But when I wasn't working, I was on the couch, disintegrating and catching up on Sara Paretsky.

Camper, the worrier, knew that something was wrong. He spent the entire summer on the floor beside that couch. He'd get up and see Jenn when she was around but he'd come back to say, "It's OK, Ann, I'm here." When I had poison ivy from head to toe, inside and out, he would go and lie beside the bath tubs full of oatmeal bath, keeping me company, letting me know that someone saw me.

He was constant comfort. Didn't say a lot. Didn't demand a lot of attention. There was a job to be done, and he was all over it.

What a good boy. He was a drooler, so Jenn had trained him to run around with a fluffy in his mouth. So, there he was, Camper and his fluffy: on guard. I slowly recovered (good shrink, good drugs, don't underestimate their importance, even if you have a good dog) and Camper went back to being Jenn's faithful dog.

So when a couple of years ago, Jenn called to say Camper had died, we both wept. Such a wonderful, charming guy, that Camper, loved to play wackamole at the Berkeley marina and chase a ball. Loved to protect the house from squirrels on the outside and bugs on the inside. Snored, just a bit, but more as the years went on. Some joint problems, you know how it is as you age. Handsome, oh, he was handsome, a true scion of his breed.

He lived a long life for a big dog, and it was clearly time for him to go when he did. But he could have lived forever as far as we were concerned. In fact he does live forever. We tell stories. We sing the Camper song and it makes Boojum really happy. We smile a lot when we talk about him, because the memory of his death is far outweighed by the wonderful stories of his life.

Did Camper go to some Elysian Field? Is there an Animal Heaven? Does he have a soul to be reincarnated — would he go up or down the ladder in terms of returning (he did have that shorthair chewing through door problem...)? Did Camper have a soul? I don't know, but I know this. He had a lot of soul. And he shared it with all of us. At the very least in our hearts and minds, Camper is on point in some big ol' field.
Goofy, happy, doing his job.

Good boy, Camper, good boy.

Rev. Ann Keeler Evans

The Rev. Ann Keeler Evans is a theologian and spiritual circuit rider for today's ecumenical world. She works with communities to create ritual for people exactly where they live — across this wide country and deep in their souls.

Poetry, prayer, public celebrations provide a bridge connecting people to the things that matter most in life. The bridge spans creed and culture and class, uniting the sacred and the secular, men and women, grownups and children, faith and its application.

At the moment she is focusing her work on weddings, but watch her blog and her store for new themes as they emerge. You can get the prayer at http://www.annkeelerevans.org/shoppe/index.php

Heaven, Hell, Whatever!

Hi: You may not want to include this in your book, because it is a little irreverent, but I can laugh about it now.

One time I moved in with this guy who had a prize Chameleon lizard. I had a cat that I loved, but the boyfriend did not.

We had gone out to dinner and while we were eating we discussed whether animals would go to Heaven when they died and agreed that they would. When we got back, the Chameleon and the cat were both gone. We had left a window open in the mobile home and assumed the cat had eaten the lizard and then got out.

I looked all over for the cat and finally figured the cat ate the lizard and it had poisoned him and he had crawled somewhere underneath and died. When I came in the house crying, I said to my boyfriend "Well, at least we know they went to Heaven." He said, "Well you can go to Hell."

So we lost a cat, a chameleon and a relationship.

Anonymous

"If I have any beliefs about immortality it is that certain dogs I know will go to heaven, and very very few people."

- James Thurber

"There is no death. Only a change of worlds."

- Chief Seattle

Photo courtesy of bubbling-well.com

Chapter 14 - Expressing Sympathy to Others

"Grief is so painfully real, regardless of its origin. The love of, and attachment to, an animal friend can equal that of human relationships. Likewise, the loss of an animal can be just as devastating."

- Rev. Joel L. Morgan

One of the toughest communications for some people is to how to offer sympathy. That is why so many people say nothing at all. It is not that they are uncaring, rather they care so much, they don't want to add to your pain or make you feel worse.

I was surprised at how many of the submissions I received talked about lack of support in the workplace. Then I remembered twenty years ago when my brother J Allen was killed in a horrible industrial accident.

Working at a local weekly newspaper at the time, my boss was also a friend and the workplace had felt like extended family. And yet, two weeks after the funeral, I was called in and told to "snap out of it."

Gordon actually looked me right in the eye and said; "Enough already! How long are you going to grieve? We have a paper to put out."

I told him that I would probably grieve for the rest of my natural life and to check back with me in a few years when he had lost someone precious to him.

Quissu

Quissu, which is Catalonian for "puppy," wasn't the first pet that I've had die during my lifetime, but she was my first dog. Being part of a "cat family" I grew up quite afraid of dogs. I'd been knocked over by an overzealous dog when I was much younger and it scared me quite a bit. Dogs were not a part of my growing up experience - and I was happy to keep it that way.

In 1999, I met my soon-to-be husband (although I am now divorced) and Quissu. While she was a very energetic dog, an 8-year-old black Siberian Husky with beautiful blue eyes, she was also the "goodwill ambassador for dogs" -- a rarity for huskies, I now know. She charmed me with the way she'd kiss you or the way she behaved with the cat. She made me laugh with her quizzical expressions and her boundless energy to chase squirrels -- that she could never catch. She could shift her eyebrows and work her "puppy dog eyes" like none other.

And she didn't just have that effect on me. My entire "cat family" soon came to know and love Quissu as well. Although she was mischievous (she once got "arrested" by the city police for being in the park a half-mile from my house, exploring by herself after jumping over the fence) she won all of our hearts.

Unfortunately, as she grew older, the genetics of being a purebred dog caught up with her. She developed a localized cancer on her front left paw that kept returning. After having the tumor removed four times, at the suggestion of the vet I finally had her leg amputated. At 13, she had to learn how to walk all over again, with only three legs. She did quite well, although I had to buy a number of throw rugs for the house as she now slid around on my hardwood floors.

As she aged, her health began to deteriorate even faster. Late last year, she developed idiopathic old dog vestibular disease: basically, she was dizzy and the vets didn't know why. She couldn't stand because she couldn't figure which way was up. Luckily, it turned out to be short-term as it lasted only a week.

Quissu just died about a month ago. While it was definitely expected, I didn't realize how much she meant to me. Knowing how much she meant to my ex-husband, I also had to do something to let him know and as we only speak through our lawyers, I had to come up with a kinder way. I finally decided to send flowers from myself and the cat, Gypsy, to let him know. I've also delivered part of Quissu's ashes, so that he can have closure in his own way. My part of Quissu's ashes are now buried under a St. Francis of Assisi statue in my backyard. It carries on my family's tradition: we've always asked St. Francis to look over our animals, even after their death.

My friends, family and especially my vet - Abri Veterinary Hospital - were all very helpful to me during this time. My mother left work to come be with me for a while and cried with me. My father helped me take Quissu's body to the vet for cremation. My vet encouraged me to cry when I called; I hadn't known what to do with her body. "We've got all the time in the world, honey. Take your time," they said.

I received cards from my family and my sister came into town to stay with me. She helped me decide what to do with Quissu's stuff and how to word the card that accompanied the flowers that I sent my ex. I received a very special card from the vet: because of Quissu's illness over the years, they'd all come to know her quite well and the entire staff had signed and written nice messages in it. When I picked up Quissu's ashes, I also received a very nice poem from the cremation service. I've also made a memorial gift to the Forsyth Humane Society in her name.

While I am very sad that she's gone, I am quite thankful that I knew her. I've attached a photo of her and Gypsy, taken about a year ago, sitting on the front porch. (It's not high quality at all, unfortunately.)

Hope this helps. Thanks for letting me share my story.

- Elizabeth

Walk with Others in Grief

If you truly want to help someone who is grieving, listen with your heart to them as they talk about their loss. They may repeat the same story over and over again as they try to process what has happened and what it will mean to them.

Keep in mind that how someone heals is unique to them and their personality, so be patient and don't invoke your own timetable on their feelings. Every person is different and is shaped by their own experiences and emotions.

As the stories have come in for this book, I am amazed how many people mentioned the sympathy cards and notes sent by friends and health care as an important part of their healing. It is a written word that can be examined in the middle of the night or left on the mantle as a reminder that others acknowledge their pain.

Condolence Card

Hi Judy,

I am responding to your request to how to respond to someone who has just lost a pet. Animals can become part of the family and sometimes live a long life, but never as long as we do, so grieving the loss of a pet is something that we have to deal with usually more than once in our lifetime. The difficult part is to deal with the lack of empathy from friends and coworkers who are not animal lovers. Those of us who have been through it don't always know the best thing to say or do, either. I would like to share one of my experiences in hopes of helping someone else in that situation.

I had a particular cat that I was very fond of. At the time, I had 3 children and a very busy life, but this pet was very cuddly and a very possessive animal. She was in good health and only 10 years old. (Many indoor cats live a much longer life) The only symptom that I noticed was that she didn't want to play with me. That's it! (I still can't believe that I took her to the vet with that symptom) They did some tests and discovered that she had cancer. Well because of her age, I decided to do everything that I could. This poor thing had chemotherapy, and two surgeries. After the first round of treatment I really thought that she would recover. But six months and $5,000 later the cancer came back and I had to make the painful decision of putting her to sleep. It was so sad to say good by to her. Very few people understood.

During the many visits to the feline oncologist, I read about different breeds of cats. I "fell in love" with the Ragdoll breed. I made a decision that would be the next pet for me. Well I couldn't find a breeder to adopt one right away, but several months later I brought home a new kitten. Although she didn't replace the one that I lost, having another full animal's life to look forward to was exciting to me.

One of the best things that made me feel good when I lost that cat was my vet sent me a condolence card with a donation to Cornell University school of Veterinary medicine in my cat's name! That touched me! The research could help other pet's live longer lives!

Nancy M. Sutherland
http://www.nancysutherland.com

The Death of My Cat, Mick

by March Bracken

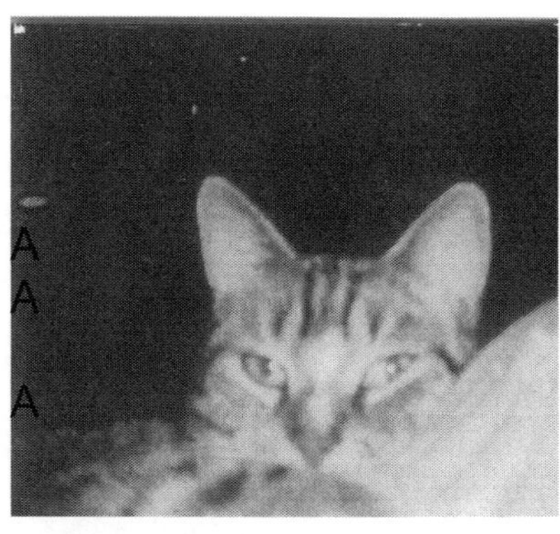

The death was quick and mean,
Pain wracking his body in spasms,
Causing him to twist, spiral in the air,
Arms and legs splayed, face contorted.
A cat in pain.
A Jesus cat.

A Jesus cat indeed,
Patiently traversing the country
Beside me in a chevy,
Baked in desert heat,
Basted in Floridian sun, and in Chicago
Icicles on the insides of frosty windows.
Purring purring purring
As the car hummed, he listened, wide green eyes attentive,
As I spun my life's story across the plains,
At times a paw on my arm as I drove,
Or a rough cat tongue licking away the tears.

This hero cat abused at birth
With his siblings in Chicago.
Ears, tails, paws lopped off by boys
Seeing humor in persecution.
Later kidnapped by devil worshippers
Into animal sacrifice.
A month later, he hobbled home,
Scorched and starved,
Dragging a broken leg
Through Santa Ana winds and toppled trees,
Honoring his commitment.
Definitely.

Definitely he was a Jesus cat,
A being who loved.
With no one else around,
He sat in the sun with a salamander,
And said "good morning" to each plant each day.
He aged with quiet dignity.
It was the cat food that
Got him in the end.
Beings baked a toxic mix in China
Where labor is cheap, and even the cat treats
Are laced with poison.
His sacred kingly being was wracked with pain.

"Get another cat," someone said. "Just get another cat."
(Getting it quite wrong, of course.)
It is the greed mongers
Who are a dime a dozen.
A truly loving soul,
Irreplaceable.

I think you will enjoy the essay submitted by Rabbi Mel Glazzer on what <u>not</u> to say to others who are grieving.

Unhelpful Responses You Will Hear From Others when Your Pet Dies and what to do About Them

© Rabbi Mel Glazer

While you're wandering through your grief after your beloved pet dies, you'll likely hear some of the unfortunate and useless comments that our society believes helps those who are in mourning over a loss. I'm not entirely convinced that most people offering them are ignorant enough to actually believe these comments help. I think that some people offering what they hope is consolation hope these comments help, even though they suspect that they don't. And I think that others buy into these myths and offer them up to grievers for lack of anything else to say. Either way, the important thing to remember is: These comments aren't true and they won't help you in any way. When you hear them, just ignore them, and try to resist getting into a debate about them with whomever offered them up. Don't waste your precious emotional energy. Just smile, nod, and ignore it all.

Here are some of some of the worst of society's responses to your loss:

1) "Don't feel bad."

You've got to be kidding. Of course you're going to feel bad, and you should. It's only natural, healthy, and emotionally honest to feel bad when you've suffered a painful loss. The only way you're going to heal is to feel bad first. If you suppress your true feelings, you will never recover. "Don't feel bad" is usually followed by another comment tailored to the situation:

- A sick pet: "...He was so sick, and he cost you so much time and money, you're better off without him."
- Any Death: "...God needed him/her more than you did."

2) Any comment about replacing your loss.

When your first pet died, what did Mom or Dad say? "Don't worry; we'll get you another one." But you didn't want another one; you wanted the one you had! When your pet dies, others may think you need an immediate replacement. They would be wrong!

3) "Why bother crying, it won't do you any good."

When you hear this comment while you're grieving your pet's death, you'll then begin to think that you're supposed to keep your feelings to yourself and that no one is interested in how you feel or in comforting you. You'll also interpret this as meaning that it's best not to speak about death or the feelings that are associated with it.

4) "Just give it time."

While time does help us heal, time all by itself will not help. It's what we do during that time that can help us heal. Thinking that time is all you need will lead you to erroneously believe that you don't have to do anything about grief, that time will take care of everything. This is as helpful as saying that if you fall down the stairs and break your arm, you don't have to do anything about it, just wait and time will heal your arm. A broken heart hurts just as much as a broken arm, and must be tended to as soon as possible. We all know people who are still mourning a loved one (or a beloved pet) who died 20 years ago, a mourner who is still waiting for "time to heal."

Time is neutral. It only heals if we engage in healing actions. Time by itself just passes.

5) "Be strong for (insert name of relative or other person)."

I can still hear my uncle saying to me right after I'd been told that my father had died, "Melvin, you have to be the man of the house now." First of all, I hardly ever saw my father during the week. He worked every day except Sunday, so I had absolutely no idea what "the man of the house" did. And, second, I was all of 12 years old. I was not a man, and didn't want to be one yet.

We all need to be needed, to feel as if our lives matter, especially after someone whose life mattered to us has died. But, to tell us to be strong for others (our families, our other pets, our friends), without allowing us to "be weak for ourselves," just doesn't work. No one should say something like this to anyone, no matter how old the mourner is.

6) "Keep busy."

Mourners are often told to keep busy so they don't have time to dwell on their feelings. This faulty advice is meant to protect us from our pain, but it never works. It just encourages us to hide from reality, to pretend that nothing is wrong. We all know from experience what happens if we do this: hiding from our feelings only postpones the inevitable confrontation with grief that we so desperately need in order to heal our hearts. The longer you hide from your feelings the more painful it will be when they finally explode out of their cave.

So what's the best response from others when your pet dies? A big hug for you, and "I'm sorry, it must hurt so bad."

Rabbi Mel Glazer
http://www.andgodcreatedhope.com

An odd by-product of my loss is that I'm aware of being an embarrassment to everyone I meet. At work, at the club, in the street, I see people, as they approach me, trying to make up their minds whether they'll say something about it' or not. I hate it if they do, and if they don't...."

- C.S. Lewis from A Grief Observed

It is often easier to say nothing than risk saying the wrong thing. However, the death of a loved one is the worst thing that can happen to someone and so to ignore the survivor, or fail to mention the loss, is to add to the hurt.

Friends and relatives need to talk about the loss and to know that they are safe in discussing it with you. They need to be reassured that you acknowledge their feelings, concerns and actions. Once you have accepted that a death has occurred and that the loved one needs your support and sympathy, there are ways to help the survivor.

- Do continue support after the funeral.
- Do listen when they need to talk about the death, person or the impact on them,
- Accept where they are and don't try to hurry them through their grief process.
- Don't compare their tragedy to someone else's or your own.
- Don't expect them to counsel and comfort you.
- Never say, "I know how you feel" because you don't. Each loss is unique.
- Do provide practical support-food, money, car rides, babysitting etc.
- Do provide social support and remind them you are available to listen and help as well as go out in public.

There are lots of ways to give verbal support and sympathy. Sympathy is the feeling or expression of sorrow for the pain or distress of somebody else. It is an understanding of someone's difficulty and ability to share their burden with compassion

Non-verbal communication is the language of relationships. If the survivor is in shock, they may not remember what you said, but will always remember what you did. Sometimes a pat on the arm, a hug, cleaning the house, raking the leaves, filling the car with gas, or writing a note lets the survivor know that you care.
These are just a few of the ways to let others know that you are aware of their sadness and acknowledge their feelings. When you offer a hand of sympathy and support, you help the survivor know they are not alone on this journey. Will it always be accepted with gratitude? No. Should you offer the hand of love and acceptance anyway? Yes. This is not about you. It is a way to honor those who have died and those who are left behind.

Self-actualizing people have a deep feeling of identification,
sympathy, and affection for human beings in general.
They feel kinship and connection,
as if all people were members of a single family.

- Abraham Maslow

Photo courtesy of petsbest.com

Chapter 16 – How Sharing Stories Helps Us Heal

Thank you so much for sharing your stories and touching the hearts of the readers. We are all connected and so your story becomes my story. My story reminds you of your own story and the stories of others you know.

Even when a loss isolates and separates us when it happens personally, we have all grieved and loss is a universal emotion. Each story is unique and individual and yet there is an underlying theme of compassion and understanding from each story teller. We see the photos and smile. We read the personal accounts and weep.

You Are in a Caring Community

People who have lost a loved one, either a human or animal, search for ways to remember that association and maintain the presence in our present lives. We strive at least keep the memory alive and pay tribute to the bond that was created. Sharing stories helps us remember those good days and the joy that loved one brought to us. We may no longer physically be able to enjoy their fun and love in this existence, but the memory can remind us of the emotions and experiences we had together.

We want to remember the deceased and maintain some part of their live lessons in our daily journey. This need to remember becomes especially strong on birthdays, anniversaries or holidays. It may be the season that triggers our memory; Or a smell, Or a treasured old toy in the attic or perhaps a bone in the yard.

Whatever the touchstone of remembering, it is therapeutic to tell a story to another person and have them acknowledge your sharing. It validates the life that was lived and honors the closeness that we felt.

Make a Mind Movie for the Listener

One of the goals of a good story is that the listener can build a picture in their mind of what you are telling them. They can actually envision this series of pictures unfolding as the tale progresses. They will, of course, put their own experiences in place as they build this inner mind movie. So, your story of your Uncle Bob taking you fishing as a child, accompanied by your beloved cocker spaniel Ruff, will star someone from their own life context.

They may very well envision a dog, but it will be one from their life experiences. They will hear your story and unfold the story in their mind of their own losses and emotions at the time. This process of hearing your story stimulates the brain to open stored memories and experiences.

That is okay that unless they knew your Uncle Bob or Ruff, they may picture another middle aged man. They may see you or perhaps themselves as the small boy. However, story is making a connection between the two of you. Your mind pictures may not be the same, but the emotions will be similar and important to both the story teller and listener.

Stories Heal the Hurt

Donald Davis, a North Carolina storyteller and teacher said, "Stories have the power to heal individuals following a significant loss because they enable us to keep alive, honor, and bless people (or animal) who are no longer with us. The story enables others to meet someone whom they will never actually meet in their lives. The story helps us process and understand our relationship with the person (or animal) whom we have lost."

Again, thank you for joining this community of kind, thoughtful people who are willing to share their innermost emotions, so that we could all benefit from their experience.

In ending, I would like to quote my friend Diane Rooks from her wonderful book: *Spinning Gold Out of Straw-How Stories Heal:*

> In the story fro Germanic mythology, Odin and his two pet ravens, Thought and Memory, reveal the vital importance of memory to give life meaning. Each morning at dawn Odin sends forth his ravens to go down, circle the Earth, and find out what has been going on. Each evening, they come back to roost, and all through the night, they tell Odin all that they've seen and heard. In this way Odin stays in touch with his universe. One dawn, having sent forth his ravens, he begins to think, "What would happen if one of the ravens should fail to return? What would I do? How could I live without both ravens?" He ponders this. In his pondering, he comes to understand that he can live without Thought but he cannot live without Memory.

May you find peace and comfort

Made in the USA
San Bernardino, CA
10 February 2015